All Our Yesterdays

All Our Yesterdays

A History of Hoarwithy
in Herefordshire

by

Elizabeth Drayson Cutcliffe

published by John Cutcliffe

Published by John Cutcliffe
in Great Britain 2009

Copyright © 2009 J. Cutcliffe

ISBN 978 0 9563894 0 4

All paper used in this publication is a natural, recyclable product made from wood grown in sustainable, well managed forests.

Artwork and Printed by Four Way Print Limited
Pennygillam Trading Estate, Lanceston, Cornwall PL15 7ED
Telephone 01566 771950

First Edition

PREFACE

My mother wrote a series of articles for her Parish Magazine Pax back in the 1990's, initially about her recollections of Hoarwithy village over the years and then when she ran out of inspiration, she took on the job of "Roving Reporter" and interviewed other "old-timers" to get their recollections as well. The last full-time vicar in any conventional sense was Reverend David Enoch, who in my humble opinion, was by far and away the best vicar I can ever remember. Unfortunately, after his untimely death, the church was down-graded and has become part of a bigger set up consisting of quite a number of churches, so that it only has services every once in a while now, with various people taking the services. Admittedly a new magazine has been born to cater for the new grouping of churches, which rejoices under the title of Phoenix, for obvious reasons; whilst mother has contributed to this in the past, it has been on an ad-hoc basis, with no theme running through it.

The reason for this book is that mother asked me about ten years ago if it would be possible to gather together all these articles and publish them as a book. I found out the details and found a printer, who said I would have to type it all up for them on a disk; so I made a start. Unfortunately, I have never learnt to type, so my typing is two-fingered and very slow. I managed to shunt my milkings (me being a herdsman) around in order to liberate myself for one or two half days a week and made a start. Then the computer centre closed, due to lack of government funding and then one of the farmers I milked for went out of cows and I had to procure some new work, which put pay to any time off; so mother's project remained on the back burner for a few years.

Recently, mother has been diagnosed as having Alzheimer's Disease, so I have downed tools to keep an eye on her and made it my number one priority to finish the book so that she can see it out in print whilst she is still compos mentis enough to enjoy the fame!

I hope people of all ages will enjoy the book and a private hope of mine is that it might be of educational value to the pupils at Kings Caple and Little Dewchurch Schools.

John Cutcliffe

HOARWITHY
Part One
Pre-War

CHAPTER ONE

The Beginning

I grew up in Hoarwithy before the last war, when life in the village was very different from today, though the sense of community still endures.

To explain how I got to Hoarwithy, I will need to go back to the beginnings of the Russill household.

My father had been training for a legal career in Newport, but having met and fallen in love with my mother, he did not relish having to wait for years until he was in a position to marry her, so cast about for another career. He loved the countryside and tried farming, but soon realised that was a very hard life even for those born and bred to it and he would stand no chance, so he thought of commerce. He had a nephew in Australia, so he and mother booked a passage and planned to marry. But the 1914 war started and the passage was cancelled (they lost their deposit) and father found himself in the army.

Just think, if it had not have been for the Great War I would be an Aussie!!

My father did apply for the Navy, but was turned down because he had had a toe amputated years previously. Why he applied, I cannot imagine as he was seasick at the sight of a rowing boat!

He joined the Army instead. His regiment had once been a mounted regiment and he was issued with a set of spurs (which I still have) and a bicycle. The training was carried out in East Anglia and mother went into lodgings at Beccles to be near him. They arranged to get married, then fate stepped in again and sent father off to hospital.

He had a septic blister on his foot (the result of army boots) and went to the M.O. who insisted on sloshing iodine all over it, in spite of father's protestations that he was allergic to iodine. Result: his foot was covered in blisters and looked terrible. He was ordered off to hospital, but was mistakenly taken to an infectious diseases hospital, where, once admitted, no one knew what to do with him except to offer him any comforts he wanted. My father asked for a hot water bottle as it was freezing in the attic where he was put to keep him away from the infectious patients. The hot water bottle did the trick, the infection drained away, and eventually, after a carbolic bath and steam sterilising of all his clothes, he was restored to the outside world, to find mother had completed all the formalities, and off they went to get married.

Poor father was in a bit of a daze and always declared he did not remember anything about it, to my mother's fury!

After their honeymoon (spent in Porthcawl in January, though I do not suppose the weather mattered!) father returned to the Army. He volunteered for the newly formed machine gun corps, and had a pretty horrible time, I suspect, but he was one of the lucky ones to survive.

In 1918 he worked in the quarter-master's stores for a time in Germany, and when he was discharged in 1919 he and mother went to live in Bosbury where he worked in a village shop to learn the grocery trade.

My mother went home to Barry to have me, to my grandmother's house, where I was born in 1920. Mother was ill after the birth and we therefore stayed there for a time. Grandmother looked after me and she believed , "If she cries, she is hungry and should be fed", (which suited me!).

Eventually we returned to Bosbury. In 1920 he and an old army friend called Frank Bufton joined forces to buy a baker's and grocer's shop in Hoarwithy, (where Olwen Topping now lives).

We came in a hired lorry, father, mother, all our goods and chattels, two dogs and lastly THE BABY riding on mother's lap.

I, of course do not remember this historic migration, but mother used to say her first sight of the village was coming down the hill from Kings Caple and seeing the houses and Church spread out in beautiful summer sunshine; the river was sparkling and covered with patches of white and gold water buttercups; and there were cattle (all Herefords in those days) standing in the water and she fell in love with Hoarwithy.

CHAPTER TWO

The Shop

Iwas a small child growing up at THE SHOP HOARWITHY. I expect, looking back, my parents had quite a hard time trying to get to grips with life in rural Herefordshire and the running of a business etc. but that did not trouble me.

A village shop in those days was one of the centres of village life and supplied everything that was required. The bake-house at the back was a hive of industry. A "modern" oven was installed fairly soon after my parents and the Bufton family took over. I can remember the furnace and the stoke-hole at one end, and the entrance to the bakery at the other, with two big wooden troughs, one at each side, in which the dough was mixed. For each trough: take one sack of flour (a hundredweight I expect) then mix up the yeast, and salt (big 7lb blocks of salt, and you cut off what was needed) then add malt from a big drum and mix together with warm water in a bucket and pour onto the flour and get mixing. The mixture was cut up in chunks and each chunk kneaded and spread out thinly one on top of the other until it was all mixed in a big heap, covered over with clean hessian, and left in the troughs with the board covers over them, to rise in the warmth until early next morning when the bakers would cut off loaf size pieces and weigh them, knead them once more and put them in tins or lay them in rounds.

Whilst the first batch was again rising the bakers would brew their tea and cook bacon and eggs etc. (in the bread oven of course!) and have their breakfast.

Then using a long-handled peel they would load the dough into the oven and leave it to bake whilst they prepared the second batch.

The smell of handmade newly baked bread was gorgeous! The old quarter sized loaf was going out of production then and the half-quarter was the norm i.e. what we think of as a standard loaf today.

The flat round loaves were stamped with a round wooden disc set with nails. This produced a distinctive pattern, and was used in days past by all bakers to indicate their loaves – a sort of trade mark.

The furnace was controlled by a damper which was shut down at night and opened in the morning to bring the two decks of the oven up to the correct heat. The heat was checked by reading the temperatures on the thermometers by the furnace doors. Does anyone remember old Walter Newport who was head baker for many years? He was a crusty old bachelor who lodged with the Owen family in their cottage near the lane up to Quarry Bank. Barbara Langford would have remembered more than I do as she grew up there. Walter would put on an old pair of spectacles and peer at the thermometer, "that there theeometer", and curse it on cold mornings when it would not rise fast enough. My father would clean out the furnace on Saturday and relight it on Sunday ready for the next week. It burned coke which was obtained from the Ross Gas Works (long gone of course).

CHAPTER THREE

The 1920's and 30's.

In the 1920's and '30's Hoarwithy was very different from today. Most of the houses were occupied by local farm workers, or tradesmen serving in the district.

The "big houses" were occupied by the local gentry: Caradoc, Kynaston, Harewood and over the river, Armstone, Pennoxstone etc.. There families lived a different life from the rest of us. They were able to employ servants for their homes and gardens etc.. Most of the big land owners had a number of tenant farmers running the farm on their estates.

Each farmer employed several, maybe half a dozen, farm workers and it was they who lived in the cottages. So, the inhabitants were predominantly farm workers, or workers such as cobblers, painters and decorators, stone masons, butcher, baker, shopkeeper, landlord of the Harp, coal-merchant, miller, etc., all working in or around the village.

People knew little about other countries and listened to ex-servicemen's views on foreigners but it was all far away and to us Gloucester or Worcester or Monmouth were a long way off. To the Russill family, a trip to visit my Grandmother and Auntie in Barry was a long journey which involved a change of trains and took three hours by rail. It is therefore understandable that to some of the older people, the inhabitants of other villages were nearly foreigners.

Our lifeline was the Great Western Railway, with Ballingham as our nearest station. In the early 1920's it boasted a Station Master and two porters. The steam trains ran between Gloucester and Hereford via Ross and went about every two hours. To go to London, some of the Gloucester trains had a special carriage which was detached and shunted onto another line at Gloucester, to tack onto the back of the London train.

All the produce of the area went out by goods train in those days – cattle, sheep, sugarbeet, milk, timber etc., and incoming goods such as coal from the Forest of Dean, and newspapers and supplies for the shop also came by rail.

Ballingham Station in its heyday had a Station Master and two porters. Horses were only just being superseded by cars and lorries then.

I recall hearing of one enterprising young man who purchased an army surplus lorry and started a "bus" service from Hereford to Hoarwithy via Holme Lacey and Ballingham. I do not know if he went on to Ross, and I think the "bus" only ran on market day. He fixed up a bench type seat on each side of the lorry and the passengers sat in two rows facing each other. It had a roof covering (presumably canvas) but no heating, lighting or cushions, so it must have been very uncomfortable.

Rumour has it that some local wag finding himself seated next to a small inoffensive lad, with, beyond the lad, a very formidable farmer's wife, put his hand around the lad and pinched the lady's bottom, whereupon she, in high indignation, slapped the face of the poor unsuspecting lad, who of course, declared his innocence and it degenerated into a near riot.

The roads in those days were unmetalled and often in an appalling state, particularly the hills which tended to resemble the stony bed of a stream. Therefore, when the "bus" came to Ballingham hill, it was, "everybody out" and after walking up the hill, they were allowed back in the "bus". It was not unknown for the passengers to have to get out and push.

The farm work was all powered by horses, and every farm had a stable full of cart-horses and a carter whose job it was to care for them and provide the right horses for use in any particular job.

My father had several horses employed in pulling the baker's carts which delivered bread and groceries to the customers. A lovely old man called Ted Gunter looked after them for us. His great grandchildren and their children living in and around the village today probably know more about him than I do.

CHAPTER FOUR

Roads

All the roads in Hoarwithy and district were constructed of stones, well rolled in by a steamroller, only main roads were tarmacked in the twenties and early thirties.

I can remember gazing at the Ross-Hereford main road (A49) in wonderment and marvelling at its tarred surface and the enormous width of it that actually allowed two cars travelling in opposite directions to pass without slowing down!!

The rural roads were covered in mud in winter and dust in summer. One could tell if a vehicle had passed in summer by the cloud of dust that hung in the air for ages after it had gone.

The potholes were filled in from time to time, as they are today!, but when it became really bad the surface would be renewed. Steam-wagons from Ross would appear and dump great piles of big stones in large heaps along the roadside and then the stone-cracker would come and do his bit.

In Hoarwithy our stone-cracker was a gentleman called "Shelty" Harris, one of the Harris family from 40 Steps, a dynasty which has only recently left 40 Steps. The old gentleman (he seemed old to me, but probably was not) used to sit on his pile of rocks and go crack-crack with his little stone-hammer and in a surprisingly short time, would reduce the big boulders (about a foot in diameter) to a neat pile of stones about 3 inches in size. I can see him now with his bread and cheese tied up in a red spotted handkerchief, sitting on the stones. He wore corduroy trousers, tied at the calf with string, and a flannel shirt, (all bought at the shop I expect).

When all was ready the roadmen of the district would form a gang and together with the steamroller crew, they would resurface the road, they would wheelbarrow loads of stone, spread them over the road and tip loose earth over them. Then the steamroller would clank backwards and forwards until it was all impacted down hard and level, then they would go on to the next bit. I enjoyed seeing this great steam monster puffing and chuffing up and down, up and down. Great fun!

When the section of the road to be repaired was finished, the roadmen went back to their own beat. Every section of the road had its own roadman then and he was responsible for clearing and maintaining the ditches and banks and hedges too in some places. Most farmers did their own hedges but the roadman saw to it that all was in his order on his stretch and he filled in potholes etc..

Mr. Lamb from Ballingham looked after the Carey side and Mr. Davies from Alma Cottage Red Rail looked after the rest of Hoarwithy. It was nice to know who was responsible (we have recently been granted the services of a lenghthman who cares for our village and several other surrounding villages as part of his beat). All the side roads and lanes were used much more in those days and were well maintained (unlike today).

From the 1920's onwards the horse was gradually replaced by motorised transport and from the thirties onwards farm stock was conveyed by lorry rather than on hoof, so slowly, the amount of manure on the roads decreased and eventually tar machines appeared with loose chippings to sprinkle on the tar and the roads slowly improved.

In the late thirties the threat of war in Europe was growing and efforts were made throughout the land to bring the roads up to standard to facilitate the movement of troops and munitions.

Floods on the road were a regular hazard in Hoarwithy. The locals accepted this philosophically and took to the higher ground when necessary. The amount of "outside" traffic was negligible then.

CHAPTER FIVE

Water

We all take our mains water for granted today, but it only came to Hoarwithy after the war - in the 60's. Before that, every house had its own arrangements for water. We at the shop were very lucky to have our own well, which was a very good one, (it still is, as Mrs. Topping can tell you). It had a pump at ground level and one put the bucket under it and worked the handle up and down vigorously and out came the water, always clear and sparkling and cold. Because it was used for mixing the dough for the bread, it had to tested at intervals and was always pronounced clean and free from germs etc.. It was tested for volume once and the verdict was that it probably came from an underground stream as the level remained constant in spite of pumping out for an hour. It was well lined with a proper circular stone wall and was about 20 or 30 feet deep as I recollect.

It was annoying to have to carry buckets into the house each morning (that was one of the chores performed by a lad) so it was up to my mother to use the water economically otherwise one of us would have to get more. The junior baker carried it up for the bread making.

The Harp and the Mill and the Aspens, or Lower Guest house as it was then, all had wells and there were systems for pumping water up to Mount Pleasant at the top of the hill and also to Altbough Farm. There was a tap along the Ballingham road from one of these systems I remember, but in spite of this, many cottages had to get their water from a brook or the river. The buckets were metal then and were quite heavy when full. Most houses had water butts for collecting rain-water from the roofs and this was used for washing and for some laundry and in the gardens etc..

I recall Sadie Pardington, the eldest of the Pardington family and my contemporary, telling mother that one washday she had had to carry ten buckets in all from the river up to their house at the top of the bank. This house is now called "Rose Cottage" and is home to Sarah Hicks.

My father, who was the member for Ballingham on the Old Ross and Whitchurch Rural District Council, worked hard to get water for the village and the original scheme drew its water from bore-holes and supplied several South Herefordshire villages but it was taken over and incorporated into a bigger water board which, I suppose, later became Dwr Cymru (Welsh Water).

When my parents retired and came here to Brae Cottage, my father constructed a concrete tank six feet square in the bank behind the house with a pipe running down to the house and they were able to get running water from the rainfall off the roof, in the kitchen and bathroom, but it never seemed to rain sufficiently to fill the tank, so he had to pay the fire brigade in Ross to come and fill the tank every so often, which became quite expensive and which probably spurred him to get mains water for Hoarwithy.

When electricity came to Hoarwithy we were all still at the shop and one of the first things father did was to get an electric pump fitted down the well to pump the water up to a big storage tank in the attic. What joy! No more humping buckets! The storage tank in the attic held sufficient water for our household needs and across to the bake-house for their needs. It was arranged that the overflow pipe came out above the kitchen window, and the switch to turn the pump on was in the kitchen, so my mother would switch it on whilst she washed up the breakfast dishes, and when the overflow came down past the window she turned it off and we were all happy all day. Olwen Topping says the tank is still there because it was too big to move.

CHAPTER SIX

Sewage

I have written about water, so I suppose the subject of sewage follows naturally. It was up to each household to make their own arrangements pre-war and for many years afterwards and I do not suppose "the powers that be" ask too many questions even today.

Many cottages had an outdoor privy and we all had the job of disposing of either the contents of the privy or buckets from the commode. We at the shop, had a system of tipping the buckets into a trench in the garden and covering it with earth until the trench was full and then digging another trench. Our garden was the land next to the church where a wooden bungalow now stands. We had our own commode indoors, and there was an outdoor toilet for the staff. It was part of the duty of the baker to empty that one.

Mr. Walter Newport, the senior baker was a character. He was a bachelor and could, at times, be quite awkward and argumentative, but he was always very polite and gallant to the ladies. When the war started, the army tried to train young A.T.S. girls to drive army vehicles, and their training route from Hereford came through Hoarwithy where they usually stopped before going back to base. Inevitably, they came looking for a toilet and poor Walter was torn between being helpful and obliging or resenting the extra work they caused him.

Some privies were cosy brick built structures with one or two (or even three) separate holes in a sturdy wooden box-like structure. All very matey. The privy was usually a little way away from the house, and often surrounded by roses or honeysuckle. Some were not so grand and were just wooden huts. Mr. Simcox who when little came often to the village with Mr. Lunt his grandfather for the fishing once lodged in my home, Brae Cottage where I now live and says there was a two-seater one at the end of the garden. Alas, gone in a landslide long ago.

Such a one was old Ned Watkins' privy which featured in the rumpus with the local foxhounds. Ned lived in a cottage on the Ballingham road and his garden and privy were situated where now stands a big new house. The hunt chased a fox down into his garden and it, with some instinct for camouflaging its scent, dashed in and dived down the hole of the privy, but the hounds were too close and followed him in and the resulting mayhem was indescribable! Ned was said to have been furious and demanded that the hunt organisation pay for a new privy (which I believe they did) and the huntsmen responsible for the hounds (or the kennel men) had the task of cleaning the hounds and were furious! The first lady to arrive at the kill flatly refused the usual privilege of accepting the brush. We do not seem to have such exciting events these days, do we?

Some people who lived near a brook or the river used quietly to empty their buckets into the water, taking good care to go downstream from the place where they drew their drinking water, but not apparently concerned that others upstream of them were doing the same thing!

Septic tanks gradually gained in popularity as water systems came along and obviously, the arrival of mains water accelerated this process.

Indoors we all had chamber-pots for night time use, which reminds me of the story that in the Harp there was great speculation at one time about a certain gentleman and his housekeeper. Did they or did they not sleep together? Then, providentially for the gossips, this gentleman had a burst pipe which flooded his bedroom and he sent urgently for the plumber to come and fix it. That evening, the plumber's mate told an enthralled audience in the Harp that he had used this as an excuse to look under the bed and had seen two chamber-pots, one each side, both of which had been used, thus proving that the two of them slept together, because, as he said, "what man would get out opposite sides of the bed and use two separate chamber-pots?"

Alas, the days of chamber-pots and privies at the bottom of the garden, with squares cut from the "News of the World" or the "Hereford Times", stuck on a nail are gone for good. The modern flush toilet with toilet rolls etc. is here to stay. THANK GOODNESS! Anyone who has had to "go", stumbling down the bottom of the garden by the light of a torch or lantern, in the middle of a cold winter's night will bless the demise of the privy!

CHAPTER SEVEN

Lighting: Part 1

Electricity came to Hoarwithy only a few months before the last war broke out and then only to the centre and the Carey Road end. The Red Rail end of the village had to wait until post war.

We all used paraffin lamps and candles. At the stores we sold candles, usually in packs of a dozen or more and paraffin oil, lamp-glasses, wicks etc. and of course any customer could order a lamp or a hurricane lantern. We carried a good stock of lamp-glasses in the cellar, on the crockery and glassware section.

The paraffin was in a square-shaped upright tank with a hand-pump on top and of course was kept outside the shop because of the fire risk. It was filled by a large, cheerful gentleman who came around with an oil tanker (once a week, I think) and carried the oil up to us in "big jugs", rather like milk churns.

The light from an old-fashioned oil lamp was a soft and gentle glow and when the "modern" Aladdin lamps came on the scene we thought they were very up-to-date. These had a mantle, similar to the gas-mantles of our town cousins, but bigger. They gave a much brighter light, but their chief disadvantage was their susceptibility to draughts and the fact that they had to hang from the ceiling or be placed in a perforated stand. They had an air intake through a central air-shaft which wafted the paraffin vapour up to the incandescent mantle and if the flame burned unevenly or too high the mantle quickly became clogged with soot and the room filled with smelly smoke. The remedy was to turn the flame down very low, and wait for it to clear itself by burning off the soot.

All lamps needed to be filled and have the wicks trimmed etc.. My mother used to do ours and I suppose the shop assistants looked after the shop lamps. In addition, we used paraffin heaters to warm the shop and we carried a heater around in the house to supply warmth upstairs, or in cold corners as needed and they too, required maintenance. The cooking was done on a two-burner paraffin stove – one for boiling and the other to heat a small oven. This cooked quite well, but was naturally slower than a modern cooker.

Looking back, I wonder how it was that we did not have more fires in rural areas, though of course we did have some. I recall Mrs. Saunders (the wife of father's partner after the Buftons left) had put a pile of clothes on the airing-rack in her kitchen and had left a lighted candle-stick on the table. They had a kitten with a fluffy tail, and this kitten (as cats will if not watched) jumped onto the table and backed into the candle which set its tail alight. It backed against a paper-bag which flared up and set the washing alight and Mrs. Saunders went into the kitchen to find it full of smoke and her clean washing smouldering. Panic! The fire was soon put out and when the kitten appeared with its tail fur singed off, the cause was revealed.

There was a real tragedy at Underhill where David and Celia Gibbs now live. Years ago two old ladies were living there and one of them was becoming senile and would wake in the night and wander around. They were both very old and frail, and it is thought that the senile one put her candle too close to the curtains and set them alight. The wood of the interior of the house was tinder dry and the whole lot went up in a fierce blaze. Someone up above heard the noise of the roof tiles cracking and sent for the fire brigade and alerted everyone to rush to help but it was a raging inferno and they could do nothing. The fire brigade took a long time to arrive and could not reach the river with their hoses when they did arrive. Think yourselves very lucky today with the modern, fast, efficient fire brigade we now have, though I see there is much indignation in the Ross Gazette that the county is talking of reducing the men and machines in Ross.

CHAPTER EIGHT

Lighting: Part 2

In the previous chapter I mentioned the existence of gas-mantles and was reminded that the younger generation had probably never seen gas lighting and would not be familiar with them. All I can say is that a gas-mantle was a small, white dome-shaped object made of a lace-like material which glowed brightly when lit from the gas-pipe. It burned but was not consumed. Sounds rather biblical does it not? (Perhaps Rev. Enoch can explain it to you!).

Pre-war, the electricity industry was not nationalised, (was anything?) and Herefordshire was served by the Staffordshire, Worcestershire and Shropshire Electric Light Company, or S.W.S. as it was known. My father very much wanted them to come to Hoarwithy as did many people; but the snag was that bringing the current here meant erecting a branch cable from the main pylons on the main road. This would cost a large sum of money, either £500 or £1000 - I forget which, but it would be about ten times more in today's currency. The S.W.S. would not pay it, we had to, so I know my father tried hard to get a group together to raise this sum, but it was not possible.

We, at the stores, were very lucky in that we had a London cousin whose husband was an electrical engineer who had been sent to Usk by the Ministry of Labour to design installations for a munitions factory. His name was Harold and he was energetic and enthusiastic and helped my father by designing an electrical layout for the stores. He and his wife came over most weekends and with his help and advice, father bought the materials needed from one of the wholesalers from whom he bought his paraffin lamps etc. and between them he and Harold wired and fitted up the stores with the idea of buying a second hand diesel generator to provide the current. Father was not having much joy in obtaining the generator, but was trying hard, when one day someone called out, "There is a strange man in your garden measuring something". Father went out and asked this man who he was and what he was doing, "Looking for the best sight for a pole", he replied,

"what for?", asks father,

"For the electricity", he replied!!

It transpired that a Mr. Hinchliffe, a retired businessman form Liverpool who had come to live in Mount Pleasant, the big house at the top of the hill, had paid S.W.S. the required sum and the electricity was coming to Hoarwithy. Great rejoicing!!

We were connected to the mains in a short while, as was the New Harp and most of the houses in the centre of the village and along the Ballingham road. Unfortunately, the Red Rail end of the village had to wait until after the war for their turn.

People came from far and near to see the "Hoarwithy Illuminations". We at the stores had a light fitted over the shop door with "Hoarwithy Stores" written on it to light the steps. The Harp had lights over their doors, and everywhere in the centre of the village lights shone in windows. Wonderful!

Our euphoria was short lived though, as it was not so many months after this that the war broke out and the blackout descended on the land.

The coming of electricity did not just give us lights. Flat irons were obsolete overnight, vacuum cleaners appeared on the scene and electric cookers replaced the old kitchen range or paraffin cooker.

Our tariff at the shop was fixed at certain level of consumption, which if exceeded, automatically put us into a much more expensive bracket. So we had to be careful and not use too many outlets at the same time. For example, mother could not run the cooker and the vacuum cleaner at the same time and if the shop lights were all on we had to be careful not to use too many house lights. Lights and power were charged separately I seem to remember. I can only suppose that S.W.S. had a limited amount of current to sell and were trying to ensure against sudden surges in demand. However that may have been, I can still remember the thrill of just clicking a switch on and off to produce or extinguish instant light on demand. Who says candle-light is romantic?

CHAPTER NINE

The Shop

My father and Frank Bufton ran the shop for about five years and then the Bufton family left and the Saunders family took their place, remaining with us for about the next ten years they too, left owing to illness (Mr. Saunders subsequently died). Father took over their share and was able to run the business himself until he sold out after the war.

I do not remember a lot about the business in the early "horse era", as my parents did not approve of children being a nuisance to customers and kept me out of the shop, but later I came to know and understand how things worked.

The bulk of the business consisted of home deliveries. My father visited a different area each day booking the orders which were then parcelled up by the shop staff and delivered by one of the delivery vans. The customers paid either the van-man or my father when he called the following week.

There were two delivery vans, each with a driver and an assistant, either a boy or a junior from the bakery and in the shop there were three shop assistants and in the bake-house two bakers. Latterly Miss West came to preside over the office and keep the accounts and do the routine office chores. She coped nobly with the food coupons during the years of Ration Books in and after the war. She lived in Ross and travelled to and from, first by train and subsequently by bus when the bus service started up in the late 1930's. She was elderly and very deaf and had to leave her previous job and so was happy to come to us. Once she got the hang of the job she was faithful and conscientious and was a real treasure. When my father was ill and had to go to hospital she came and slept in to give mother support.

The vans from Hoarwithy Shop delivered far and wide: Hoarwithy itself, Hentland, Harewood End, Orcop, St. Weonards, Llanwarne, Kings Caple, How Caple, Fawley, Brockhampton, Carey, Ballingham, Bolstone, Little Dewchurch, Sellack, Foy, etc..

The housewives from many of the more distant homes and farms never actually came to the shop and relied on my father's weekly visits to order their groceries and to keep up to date with happenings in the district. Many treated him as a trusty friend and sought his help and advice. He took to issuing a monthly letter which gave information on products as well as news. These were cherished by some who probably received very few letters.

Inevitably the shop was one of the local meeting places and the centre for local affairs. Everyone knew everyone in those days and many were related by ties of blood or marriage. It was a great place for gossip and scandal, but equally, village people were ready to help in times of trouble and we all felt we "belonged".

To illustrate this, I recall a certain lady who worked on an isolated farm as housekeeper. The farmer's wife had died and he had several grown sons who worked the farm and needed domestic help badly. She, inevitably, became pregnant and arranged to marry one of the sons, but by the time all was organised, time had caught up with them and the baby had already arrived, so she asked father to make her a combined wedding/christening cake. This caused much discussion as to the correct decoration etc. but before the work could start on it the lady had a blazing row with the father and left the district with the baby (to my father's relief!).

We had a telephone, but few people had one in those days and in emergencies we often had to pass on messages, or father would have to turn out to help people. I can recall vividly when Mr. and Mrs. Owen (Barbara Langford's parents) were called to Hereford Hospital where their little daughter Betty was very ill. The call came in the late evening and father took them to hospital and brought them back with the sad news that the little girl was dead. I am sure Barbara remembers all too clearly the grief and shock that caused.

So you see life was and still is, a mixture of farce and tragedy.

CHAPTER TEN

General Stores

The term "General Stores" really did cover most things. As well as groceries, the shop stocked clothing and drapery. We sold a limited collection of women's dresses and lengths of dress materials for sewing at home, with such ancillary items as sewing cottons, needles, pins, elastic, fancy trimmings, cards of white cotton-covered buttons etc..

Underwear for ladies consisted of knickers (known in the trade as divided skirts and by the flippant as bloomers or passion killers) and petticoats and stocking. The principal fabric was "artificial silk", or rayon to give it its proper name.

The stockings were black wool for old ladies and school children and lisle (a cotton/rayon mixture?) or the so-called silk stockings which were of rayon for adults.

For little girls there were jumpers and skirts and in summer white socks and cotton dresses (many home-made). Women's overalls and pinafores of cotton, usually the wrap-around sort were worn by nearly all females.

For men it was corduroy trousers and flannelette shirts and for Sundays, cotton shirts with detachable collars etc. and of course handkerchiefs, both white and the red-spotty kind. There were woollen socks for men, and for boys the knee-high socks, grey with coloured bands around the tops. Boys had short trousers, usually grey flannel and woollen jerseys. Men had long-johns and boys had short underpants. Boots and wellingtons were the usual footwear. I do not think we stocked these, but they could be ordered if wanted.

I expect there were other items of clothing which I have forgotten.

CHAPTER ELEVEN

The Hoarwithy-Kings Caple Bridge

The original bridge was built of wood; chestnut I believe and rumour has it that when it was replaced by the old toll bridge many of the timbers were sold off and used locally. Someone told my father that the big beams in the attic of the shop (where Olwen Topping now lives) came from the old bridge.

The shop originally had a third storey which was taken down and the attic was constructed with these big beams to strengthen the structure. I cannot vouch for the truth of all this of course, but I can say definitely that pre-war there were some old wooden baulks of timber in the water below the toll-house end of the bridge, which could well have been remnants of a wooden bridge.

There was a high gate across the road by the toll-house and pre-war an old lady living in the toll-house had the job of collecting the money. I think it was a penny (or maybe 2d) for pedestrians and 3d for motorbikes or pushbikes and 6d for carts, cars or vans; one way of course.

She was very conscientious about collecting the tolls, so I presume her livelihood depended on the amount she obtained. She was a tiny little thing, her hair scraped back into a tight bun and she seemed to me like a little old witch. Probably she was not old at all, just thin and worn. I do not know what she charged for animals, but I guess it would be something.

I know the Scudamores who lived at Ruxton had a foxhound puppy once, which they were rearing for the hunt. This animal used to hang around and sneak through when the gate was opened for someone. He had discovered that there was very nice bacon at the shop and had managed once or twice to creep into the cellar and have a feed. Father asked "Lady Bridge", as we called her, to stop him getting past.

She did so but reported that when shooed away he went down the bank and swam across. (I told you in a previous episode that shop bacon tasted very nice, did I not?). The old lady's field-day was the annual point-to-point races at Fawley when dozens of cars came across from all over the county, and of course, back again. She usually left the gate open from about 10pm when she went to bed, but not if she thought a car was going to return.

Father had business in Fawley and How Caple one day and from there he had to go on into Ross. Of course he returned home via Rig's Wood and Red Rail. He was amused to notice that when he went to bed, the light on the bridge was still burning and she was up waiting for him.

A strong movement arose (in the late 30's I think) that the county council ought to buy out the bridge owners and abolish the tolls. The Kings Caple inhabitants were not so dependent on the bridge as they are now because they did have their own Post Office, but all the same many people had to cross the river to work in both directions and the tolls were irksome.

Father delivered groceries "across the river" and many of his workforce lived in Kings Caple. There was Mr. Woods who managed the shop itself at one time, Bill Tombs from The Clusters, the number one van driver and Jimmie Ravenhill and Iris Ravenhill who helped mother. I remember Albert Bridge and Don Campbell both of whom worked in the shop at various times. No doubt other people on both sides of the bridge employed workers who lived "across the water". The petition was eventually successful and the tolls went after a prolonged battle.

More recently, as most of you remember, the metal toll bridge became unsafe and the present bridge was built. Everyone realised then how important our bridge is, when for six weeks it was not there and Kings Caple people particularly had to go all the way into Ross to cross the river. Incidentally have you noticed how much the bed of the river has shifted? The central piers are not central anymore and the buttress on the Kings Caple side is high and dry and on the Hoarwithy side the path underneath the bridge has gone and the water is right up to the toll-house buttress.

To digress and return to the point-to-point races. One year when all the cars started to arrive they found a meadow near the racecourse with the gate open and a large notice "Car Park 2/6" and a man taking the money as they drove in. During the meeting a local farmer happened to meet the owner of the field and said, "I am surprised at you allowing the race-goers to park on your field, I thought you had it down to hay".

"What!", said the owner, rushed off to look and found his field full of cars and no sign of the car park attendant anywhere.

No-one could recall who he was and no-one had given him permission of course. So, some smart confidence trickster got away with it and the farmer had his hay crop ruined.

CHAPTER TWELVE

Hoarwithy Sports

I would like to tell you about Hoarwithy Sports and the FAIR. As a small child it was magical for me and it was the highlight of the year for Hoarwithy until the war and I am afraid I cannot remember when it ceased.

I know the Fair arrived every summer, and the thrill of watching the big steam wagons and the gypsy caravans turning into the meadow and settling in, erecting all the stalls and "rides" was quite wonderful. Particularly the roundabouts! It was lovely to see it gradually taking shape. There was the organ with its figurines playing loud mechanical tunes and all those gorgeous horses and ostriches, all painted in bright colours and each with a brass pole to hold onto. They were so stately as they moved up and down, all of them galloping around and around! There were lights and mirrors and gilding everywhere. It was perfect heaven for a small country child.

I liked the swing-boats and the stalls and the hoop-la and the coconut shies etc., but the roundabout was my favourite.

In the mornings it was exciting to wander around the field and look at the gypsy caravans and watch their comings and goings. They were real Romany gypsies, not the tinkers and "New Age Travellers" of today. Their caravans were painted in bright colours and furnished with cut-glass and plush and velvet curtains, brass ornaments, lace ruffles, etc.. Everything was bright and clean. The caravans were pulled by gypsy ponies. The women were sturdy, sun-burnt with layers of petticoats, and the men dark and agile, jumping on and off the roundabouts, or stoking boilers etc.. All very romantic.

The sports consisted of races (I am not sure who organised them) and were popular with the young and athletic, but since I was not athletic I did not do anything there.

The whole thing lasted, I think, about three days, finishing with a grand Saturday night finale. I could hear all the music and noise from my bed. I think it went on until about midnight. The next week they all dismantled their rides, packed up and pulled out.

For those who do not know, the sports meadow is the big meadow at the back of the New Harp.

CHAPTER THIRTEEN

The Shop Again

Much of the food in the shop was actually weighed and wrapped in the shop itself, often in printed packets with slogans such as "Best Burmese Rice" or "Fine Quality Ceylon Tea", etc. but in the country as a whole there was a big government campaign being waged to persuade customers to "Buy British". I think this was aimed largely at manufactured goods in the hope of combating cheap foreign imports.

One day, the girls working in the shop had a packet of rice returned to them from a customer with a message saying, "We do not want any of this foreign rubbish. We demand British rice"! Perplexed, they asked my father for guidance. He promptly tipped the rice from the packet into a plain bag, and said, "Send it back with a note that this is British rice". The customer was quite happy with that!

Greengrocery, apart from oranges and bananas and a few onions perhaps, was not a selling line, as most customers grew their own vegetables and fruit.

The ordinary working family could not afford to buy what they could grow in their own gardens. Fruit was made into jam, or else bottled (Kilner jars were just coming into being before the war) and surplus fruit and vegetables were given to neighbours as needed. Runner beans could be salted down and carrots, potatoes and apples etc. stored for the winter. (Do not forget, no electricity, no deep freeze!).

I expect local produce was sent to be sold in the town shops. In fact, some farms did grow soft fruit. I recall seeing rows of blackcurrant bushes on the Aramstone fields being picked up by local women, for sale – possibly to a jam factory? Mr. Alford, who lived in Kings Caple, used to grow and sell strawberries. Mother would buy a big punnet of them once a year, with which to gorge ourselves. They were lovely! Juicy and sweet and, by today's standard, cost very little.

But to return to the shop! No freezers – therefore no ice-cream. That was a real treat and reserved for trips to town or outings to the seaside.

On the positive side, we did a steady trade in tinned fruit: peaches, apricots, pears and pineapples and for summer drinks, we sold lemonade powder or crystals for making orange syrup, etc..

Sunday tea was more of a ritual then: bread and butter and home-made jam, tinned fruit and custard, trifles, lots of different home-made cakes and tarts. In winter perhaps sausage rolls and in summer home boiled ham and salad. Sardines or salmon (tinned of course) were also favourites. Much of this was bought from the shop, of course.

Sunday was the day to dress up and go visiting and after the sumptuous tea the family and visitors might go to Evensong at the local church.

When I was small, we had a baker, I recall, who was also a pastry cook and he used to make some pastries and cakes for the shop, which were bought with great satisfaction by those who could afford them – such things as cream horns, jam turnovers, chesterfield cake, etc. and at Christmas he would make about a dozen or more Christmas cakes. These were all beautifully decorated with sugar flowers etc. – each one different and of a unique design. I can remember being asked to go and look at them. I suspect these cakes were probably ordered in advance, as I do not think they could be just made on the off chance of someone buying them.

One Christmas this man entered a competition in Hereford (and won it I believe) by making Cinderella's coach and icing it and attaching two white horses, scrounged from a "White Horse" whisky window display. He covered these with marzipan and icing sugar and it was apparently a real work of art.

Dough cakes were a regular feature for many years and all the bakers over the years would make a few for sale each week. They were made from ordinary bread dough with the addition of mixed fruit, spices and sugar, and were very tasty! Later on the factory-made Lyons and Scribona goods appeared – Swiss rolls, sponge cakes, cup cakes, fruit pies, etc. and we had a small but steady demand for them.

Biscuits, then, came in square 7lb tins and had to be weighed out in 1/2 lbs or whatever quantity was needed. We had a stack of biscuit tins in front of the counter, and the top tier had glass lids fitted over them so that the customers could see them and decide which sort they wanted. There was not much choice – there were Marie, Osborn, custard creams, etc..

Oranges came in big sturdy wooden crates, like a bedside locker. The one side was levered off with a crowbar, and the box propped up so that the customers could see and select the oranges they wanted. Usually a box of oranges would be propped up against the counter. The usual price, unless they were big Jaffa oranges, was seven for 6d.

One year there were some orphaned lambs (known as tiddlers) in the field opposite the original Post Office, now "Evergreen". I had fed one of these from the bottle and it must have followed me one day and it came into the shop and helped itself to an orange. It became a real menace and helped itself whenever it felt like it. It was a fully grown sheep by now and I can see my father heaving it bodily out of the shop and down the steps to the road where it shook itself and turned and charged right back up again. I think at this stage Phil Williams carted it off to market and peace was restored.

The granary out at the back was stocked with various mixtures of corn and grain for poultry and animal feed. I recall maize and different grades of chick feed and biscuit meal etc., etc..

The cellar had shelves of glass and crockery – tea-sets, glass tumblers, lamp glasses, teapots, jugs, etc., etc.. There was a meat-safe for keeping sides of bacon, a barrel of vinegar, and also stacks of general groceries awaiting their turn to be unpacked.

Sugar was stored upstairs in an alcove on the ground floor (too cold and damp in the cellar).

I hope all this gives some idea of the range of goods stocked by a country shop.

Many wholesale firms issued catalogues from which one could order goods not normally in stock, e.g. a new cooking-stove or paraffin heater, a hip-bath. You think of it and Hoarwithy Shop could probably procure it for you!

CHAPTER FOURTEEN

Shopping

Iwonder why it is that whenever I go shopping in the supermarket I always seem to get a trolley with a mind of its own. Whilst wrestling my way around I was thinking back to pre-war shopping days in father's shop and wondering if we have really progressed very much. I grant you that now we can buy all sorts of things that were unobtainable then (or even unheard of) but I question whether the general quality of foodstuffs is much improved and customers do not have a grocer call on them in person for their order and then deliver it to them each week.

Today's groceries and foodstuffs come to the shops already packed and labelled by and large, but pre-war, with a few exceptions, everything came in bulk and had to be unpacked, weighed and packaged up ready for sale. The exceptions were Tate and Lyle who had started packaging granulated sugar in 2lb bags and margarine, which was of course a manufactured product, was packed in ½lb packets. It was either Stork or Blue-Band and was generally considered a very inferior product to butter. Butter came in 56lb blocks, mostly New Zealand and had to be cut into layers with a wire and then each layer was cut into cubes with a large knife and weighed and packed in greaseproof paper (which itself came in sheets and had to be cut to size). Weighing butter was quite fiddly as it usually meant adding or subtracting a small piece to get the precise 1lb or ½lb weight to each packet.

We also sold home-made butter, which came already weighed from our customers. Many farmer's wives made butter with any surplus milk from their cows and were glad to sell it to father. A slice of our shop bread, made by our own bakers, with a generous spread of farm butter, made a meal very much worth having.

Cheeses came (as one sees in cheese shops today) in large rounds wrapped in butter-muslin. They had to be skinned, cut in half and then quarters with a cheese-wire and then displayed to the public. Customers took it for granted that they could taste before buying.

Dried fruit came in boxes and had to be washed, sieved and inspected for twigs, nails, grubs etc. before being weighed and bagged into dark blue or purple bags.

Rice and sugars such as Demarera or moist brown sugar, tapioca, tea and coffee beans all came in sacks or boxes and had to be weighed and wrapped. Tea, of course, came packed in foil-lined tea-chests. some firms produced cardboard cartons with slogans such as "Best Burmese Rice" or So and So's Prime Tea etc. and for a small extra charge the grocer buying them could have his name and address printed on the packets as well. These were quite easy to open up and then fold the bottom ends in and add the tea, or rice, or whatever, and then fold down the tops.

As you can see from this, the shop assistants spent a lot of time packaging products and making up the grocery orders which my father had collected, ready for the van-men to take out and deliver, so that, even if there were not many customers actually in the shop, they were always busy. There was quite an art in packing groceries (not all heaved into plastic bags higgeldy - piggeldy like today). Mr. Wood, who held sway in the shop latterly insisted on the girls packing everything neatly - big things to the bottom and more fragile goods to the top and soap etc. packed where it could not taint food. There might well be such items as a can of paraffin or sugar and probably contained a few tipsy wasps was not very nice.

My father decided to weigh up just a few packets at a time and to put the sack of sugar in a sealed tea-chest to protect it. The inevitable happened one Saturday evening when the shop was crowed with customers and all the staff were working hard. Some lady came in and asked for ½lb of demarera and the fixture was empty, so my father levered off the lid of a sealed chest with the shop crowbar to get it for her. Now, unfortunately, unknown to everyone, there was a small knot hole at the back of this chest and the wasps had been getting in for a while, but were unable to get out again and when father raised the lid there was a mighty WHOOSH as a great swarm of tipsy wasps erupted into the shop and in two seconds flat my father found himself completely alone in an empty shop.

Order was eventually restored and business resumed. As my late husband would have said, "Never a dull moment".

More about other pests another time.

CHAPTER FIFTEEN

Education: Part 1

Hentland School was the local village school for most of the Hoarwithy children, though some, like myself, went in the opposite direction to Ballingham School. They were both Church of England schools then, as were most of the schools in South Herefordshire.

I believe the schools' governors were responsible for the fabric and the county education authority for funding the teachers and paying for the equipment.

The parish priest had a say in appointing the teachers and was responsible for the religious education. Some came into the schools and actually taught the children, but I think most of the vicars, like Ballingham's Rev. Norcock, were content to let the teachers do the teaching and just visited the school from time to time and quizzed us.

Each day started with prayers, a hymn and a reading and then we had a scripture lesson for the first teaching period. Someone on high issued a syllabus each year and we learned our catechism, which we gabbled off parrot-fashion and then certain prayers, bible readings and sections of the prayer-book etc. and then we had a visit from an inspector who tested us on what we had learned.

The rest of the school day was devoted to the 3R's and geography, history, handwork etc..

The pupils were divided into roughly three sections. The infants up to about six years old had a separate room and were taught by an uncertificated teacher (or monitor) and the juniors, up to about nine years and the seniors, up to fourteen years, when they left school were taught by The Teacher. Teacher would give one group some work to do, sums, reading etc. whilst she taught the other group and vice-versa.

The infants used slates and slate pencils, as exercise books were not issued until the junior class (they were used sparingly because of the cost).

The infants learned to count with help of a big bead frame and would chant the numbers in a chorus and soon learned to count from one to a hundred. Next they learned adding and subtracting by watching the beads being moved across the frame.

Spelling was learned slowly by acquiring the letters of the alphabet one by one and being given cardboard letters with which to try and form words written on the blackboard.

In the juniors, one had to learn multiplication and division and spelling (followed by the dreaded dictation tests!) and cope with problem questions such as:- add the price of two and a half yards of cloth at 9d a foot and two and three quarter pounds of apples at 5 1/4d a lb and work out in £,,s,,d how much change you would have from nine shillings. (Do not ask me – I was never very good at arithmetic!).

There were not a lot of textbooks and pupils often had to share, two children to a book, but as there were not many of us we did get more individual attention than is perhaps the case today.

Handicrafts consisted of sewing and knitting for the boys. How I wished I could have joined the boys! We learned different types of seams, run and fell, French seams etc.. Each seam had to be pinned , tacked and then stitched (by hand of course – there were no sewing machines then). We learned various embroidery stitches to decorate the garments we made. We also learned hoe to make lace insertions and scalloping etc.! Knitting was a struggle for me. We started with dish-clothes and graduated to socks (four steel needles now!) but I left school before I got to the heel, so I never learnt how to "turn a heel".

At the age of ten or eleven we had to sit a test to qualify for secondary education. If we were good enough, we could go to Ross Grammar or Hereford High School for boys or girls. About 90% of pupils could not avail themselves of this chance even if they had passed because their parents could not afford to keep them in school after the age of fourteen, which was the leaving age.

Most boys left and went to work on the farms or as gardeners etc. on the estates of the landowners and the girls went into domestic service. A few were lucky and got jobs in town. My father had no problem in obtaining staff for the shop, or the delivery vans, or the bakery, as you can imagine.

I was one of the lucky ones and passed the scholarship exam to Hereford. I went to the Girls' High School and I lost touch with the village school, but I will tell more about school playtimes, social events etc., in the next chapter.

CHAPTER SIXTEEN

Education: Part 2

Rural schools gave children a good start in life and were in many ways superior to city schools with their much larger classes. Mostly, the country schools were run by dedicated, hardworking teachers who really knew their pupils and their families and strove to bring out the best in everyone.

In Ballingham, we worked during lesson time but had no homework afterwards. We were, however, encouraged to read library books. The County Library in Hereford sent a large wooden crate, which was changed each term, to each school. We were encouraged to read for pleasure from these library books. We had certain periods in school for reading and we also read in our own time. We each had a notebook in which we recorded the title, author and page number each time we had a reading lesson. The only rules were: you always washed your hands before taking a book and you had to finish one book before going on to another. The boxes of books were obviously filled with care and were graded from simple fairy stories up to English classics, thus suiting all ages.

The school day was divided by two short breaks, one each in the morning and afternoon and a much longer dinner hour. During the breaks we ran around and let off steam in the playgrounds (we had two). We played such games as "What's the time Mr. Wolf?", "Sheep, sheep, come home", "Statues", "Round and round the Mulberry Bush", "Oranges and Lemons" and many others.

The dinner hour was truly our own and we had complete freedom to go where we liked and do as we liked. Teacher went home to dinner and we ate our sandwiches and drank our cold tea or lemonade as quickly as we could. (No school dinners then!).

Sometimes we played around the ponds, gathered frog spawn, or went bird nesting, picked flowers or played games.

The senior pupils often organised a game of Fox and Hounds in which we all joined. Two children were chosen as foxes and given five minutes by the school clock to vanish. Then the rest in descending order were picked as master, assistant master, chief whip and second whip, helper first lady and then the other huntsmen and women. The smaller children were picked as chief hound, leading hounds etc.. We all trotted off then after the foxes. When stumped, we would all shout loudly:-

"If you don't holler
We won't follow"

And then the foxes were then obliged to shout and off we would go. We generally caught them, but occasionally a fox escaped. The huntsman who caught a fox chopped off the head and tail (in mime of course) and presented the brush to the first lady to arrive. We usually finished in time to get back to school before the bell was rung.

The country code as it is known today was something which was naturally instilled into us and we in turn handed it down to the younger ones and we grew up just knowing the do's and don'ts of life without consciously learning it. We all knew that you shut a gate behind you, you do not run through growing crops, you can pick up windfalls quite legitimately but you do not pick growing fruit (I am not saying one did not sometimes give a shake to an apple or pear tree!). It was quite legitimate to collect birds' eggs but you did not frighten the birds and you were allowed to take only one egg per nest. I expect, with hindsight, the villagers all knew us and watched what we were doing and would not have hesitated to intervene if we had misbehaved.

Our teacher had a cane, but it was rarely used though it had a deterrent effect. I can only remember it being used for really blatant insolence or misbehaviour.

Miss Jones, our teacher, was a good lady and thoughtful of our welfare. She got the sewing class on to making felt slippers out of old hats, and then, when children were soaked in a downpour, she would dry their clothes and shoes by the fire and give them slippers to wear. She also started a scheme for us all to have a cup of hot cocoa at midmorning during winter. Those who could afford it paid 2d a week and she provided the cocoa, milk and sugar. The senior boys made it and kept it hot on the stove for us.

The infants' room had an ordinary big fireplace and the main schoolroom had a cast iron stove. The junior teacher lit these fires early before we arrived and we usually had a nice warm school. The stove tended to smoke sometimes when the wind was a certain direction, which was not so nice. In the cloakroom , we had a metal washstand with a bowl, with a bucket beneath to collect the water when we removed the plug. It was filled from a big enamel jug. The toilets were across the playground – the usual type of thing, wooden bench with round holes and a pit underneath. For drinking water we had an earthenware cylinder with a tap at the bottom, but any water which emerged tasted so foul we preferred to stay thirsty. (One sees them in antique shops these days – So and so's Patent Water Filter. They make me shudder!).

Country schools probably cost only a fraction to run in comparison with schools today and we were no doubt naïve and unwordly by today's standards, but we had a good grounding in the basics of education and of life, so do not underestimate the country bred children of that era!

CHAPTER SEVENTEEN

In Sickness and in Health: Part 1

Before the formation of the National Health Service people thought twice before going to the doctor. Doctor's bills had to be paid!

Workers were paid something towards medical treatment and when off work with a sick note from the doctor, they were "on the panel". I never quite understood what that was but I assume they were entitled to some sort of sick pay. This did not, however include their families.

There was some scheme in Hoarwithy and district by which folk paid a few pence each week towards the district nurse. She then visited and cared for the sick and also delivered babies and cared for them and their mothers. Again, I am unsure whether she was able to care for all who asked for her or only those who subscribed.

There was a doctor in Ross called Dr. Green (no relation to the late Dr. Green of Western-under-Penyard) and another in Much Birch, a Dr. Mc Michael who was followed by Dr. Mc Ginn (the father of the late Dr. Mc Ginn who was killed in a car crash) and these two doctors both held sessions in Hoarwithy for half a day a week.

All patients were charged for their consultations and for the medicines they received. At that period all doctors had quite extensive dispensaries attached to their surgeries and would have all medicines, pills, ointments etc. assembled for their patients either during surgery or later the same day.

Chemists sold their own and factory made patent medicines for all sorts of illnesses and were then, as now, well patronised by the general public.

In my father's shop we sold aspirin, cough mixture, Epsom-salts, senna pods, "Carters' Little Liver Pills", something called "Slippery Elm" (what that was for, I never discovered) and other patent medicines, also bandages and cotton wool and iodine. At that period iodine was the disinfectant for all cuts, sores, bruises etc.. There were also Glauber Salts for animal use (or possibly human?) and others which I cannot now recall.

In spite of the growing market for patent medicines, many of the older generation still preferred to try their own remedies and elderflower tea was a very popular cure for many ailments, as were other herbal remedies I expect. Elderflower tea was supposed to cure everything from 'flu to in-growing toenails. It was and no doubt still is, a good remedy for feverish illnesses. People would say, "Go to bed with a hot brick and good dose of elderflower tea and sweat it out and you'll be better by morning".

If somebody was seriously ill or suffered an accident such as a broken bone or deep cut they had to go to the doctor and face up to the bill which would accrue. In those days, many doctors tended to charge according to one's means. Thus if the patient was a prosperous farmer (?) – yes, there were some! or a tradesman, the bill might be in guineas, but if the patient was a pensioner trying to live on 10/- (50p) a week old age pension, the bill might be in pence or a few shillings and most doctors did not push too hard for payment

It was amusing to notice that Dr. Green, who was an ex-army doctor from World War 1 and had no time for malingerers, was considered a very good doctor who did his best for all his patients and was the preferred doctor for serious illness, whereas Dr. Mc Ginn, who was perhaps too kind-hearted, was the doctor to approach if you wanted time off work. Patients could go to whichever doctor they wished; there was no system of registration as there is today.

It so happened that my father called on Mrs. Mc Ginn at Much Birch for her grocery order on the same that the medicines for the Hoarwithy patients seen in the Hoarwithy surgery were made up and so the system came into being that the bottles, packets etc. were put into a box ready for him to collect and take back to the shop from whence the patients collected them. Bearing in mind that people had to cycle or walk to Much Birch this was a great help.

My father observed that Dr. Mc Ginn seemed to have three standard medicines – a brown one, a red one and a clear one with a large amount of white powder in the bottom of the bottle. The last one was probably for indigestion. On one occasion the cork worked loose from one of the bottles and when he arrived home father found that most of the clear liquid from the indigestion mixture had leaked out. He knew the old lady for whom it was intended was real hypochondriac so he filled the bottle with water and hoped it would do no harm. He telephoned Dr. Mc Ginn to explain and was told that he had done the right thing. The following week the doctor told him that the old lady had noticed the difference and had declared it was much better than the usual medicine and had done her a lot of good and why could not she have it always?

There were many outbreaks of infectious diseases and also deaths from tuberculosis, diptheria etc. but this is another chapter.

CHAPTER EIGHTEEN

In Sickness and in Health: Part 2

In the last chapter I wrote about local doctors and the care they gave to Hoarwithy people and this started me thinking of how much the medical world has progressed since then. The emphasis today is on preventative medicine and we all benefit from it. Mothers expect to have their babies immunised against all sorts of illnesses, holidaymakers seek immunising from tropical diseases as a matter of course and we "oldies" demand our 'flu jabs etc.. Babies born today are examined and checked for any birth defects which are promptly corrected. We expect that antibiotics and many other powerful drugs should be available to us as needed. We are constantly deluged with advice on all sorts of dietary and exercising regimes.

None of this happened in my childhood. The new sulphonamide drugs were being developed just before the war and surgery was being developed just before the war and surgery was in the ascendancy. Surgeons rushed in and operated on all sorts of conditions that today would be treated by drugs and other more conservative means. Operations for cancer, tonsils, piles etc. are just a few of the things which, with hindsight, were probably not the wonderful cures people thought they were at the time.

Complaints such as arthritis, bronchitis and pneumonia and children's infections such as measles, mumps and chickenpox were nursed and relieved by medicines, embrocations etc. but there were no miracle cures. With regard to childhood illnesses, sometimes the schools closed down and hoped that, with the children scattered around in their homes, the infection would soon run its course and the epidemic would stop. Diphtheria was a serious illness which most mothers dreaded. It was not that common, but serious outbreaks did occur and there were some deaths as a result.

Vaccinations for smallpox were given to most babies. This had been obligatory by law for some years and had stopped the disease by the time I came along, though my grandmother had had it when she was a teenager.

Tuberculosis was quite common, and people went to hospital to be treated. The cure was fresh air, good food and rest in bed and more fresh air. The wards were unheated and open to the air on one side. Before then many people nursed their relatives in a hut in the garden. I can vaguely remember going to "The Salmons" to see some lady who was being nursed in a wooden hut at the back of the house. If the patient did not survive, I suppose it at least prevented the spread of the infection. When large families were all crowded together in small cottages it was asking for trouble if one member caught tuberculosis and was not diagnosed and promptly removed.

As I have said, the correction of defects was not undertaken as a matter of routine as it is today and deformities of many sorts were seen here and there. I was talking to

David Gibbs (our village wizard of the pensions and insurance fame) recently and he asked if I knew why his office was called the donkey house. I did not know why it was so called, but as soon as he mentioned "donkey" I remembered that a family called Bundy had lived there some years ago and Mr. Ned Bundy had had a club foot which made him very lame and he therefore used a little donkey-cart to go about his daily business, whatever that was and the snug little stone building by the gate where David now earns his living was obviously the home of the donkey and its cart.

Squints! One hardly sees anyone with a squint today, but I can recall at least two ladies with the most ferocious squints in the district. As a child, I used to fascinated by them and wonder which eye was actually looking at me and what they saw with the other eye and how they managed to sort out the two different views at the same time!

Teeth! Some of the older folk had none and most people had some gaps. False teeth did tend to look like tombstones and people endured toothache until they finally "had it out"! There was not much filling of teeth done then – it was probably too expensive to undertake anyway. In the schools, a dentist visited the children (once a year, I expect) but all he did was extract rotten teeth. He did carry a horrible metal wheel – very big and heavy, which I now realize was a hand-cranked device for drilling teeth, but which we all regarded with suspicion as some implement of torture, which, fortunately, he never used. I recall my mother asking if he could straighten my teeth because they were crooked and overcrowded, but she fobbed off with, "She'll grow out of it". I did not of course and years later I was told by a private dentist that much could have been done if I had come to him when I was younger. Dental care did not extend to the secondary schools and parents were expected to send their children to private dentists.

Then, of course, there was the school nurse who visited us regularly. She was I think, the district nurse and schools were a part of her job – though she may have been employed by the Education Department, I do not know. She saw us all, one at a time and inspected our heads for lice, and checked that our knickers were clean and that we had washed our hands and our necks etc.. I do not know what else she was looking for. She was a nice gentle lady and did not cause panic like the dentist.

Babies were mostly born at home, delivered by a doctor or district nurse and the new mother was rested in bed and cared for by the family, unless she had a lot of children to care for and no relatives to help. Most country families helped one another then, as now, so I expect most newborn babies and their mothers received adequate care.

My mother, having had a bad time when I was born, opted to go into Ross to a private nursing home to have my brother who arrived four years after me. Father said it scared him to death because the midwife would say, "Oh! Mr. Russill now that you have come to visit your wife, I'll pop out for a while – there is no one else expected to arrive this week, so you'll be all right" and she would walk off down the town leaving him having nightmares about what he should do if some heavily pregnant lady suddenly appeared and expected him to know how to deliver her baby.

I think this has given you some idea of medical care as it was before the war and perhaps made us all appreciate that the N.H.S. for all its imperfections, is not so bad after all.

CHAPTER NINETEEN

Religion (As it was)

Hoarwithy in my childhood had a church and also a flourishing chapel. I do not think the chapel belonged to any specific nonconformist group, but was run by and for a group of local people. Mr. Aubrey Roberts from Bromley Court was prominent amongst them and also the Sherrat family from Prothither and Miss Mailes and the Williams family from the Post Office etc..

There were a few Roman Catholic families in the district. In those days the village folk tended to think that Catholicism was somehow a bit alien and exotic and Catholics did not of course mingle with any other religions then. There was some limited contact between church and chapel amongst adults and some children tended to change allegiance from one Sunday School to the other according to the prospects of Christmas parties or summer outings.

Since my parents were Baptists by upbringing (in fact it was as Sunday School teachers in a Baptist chapel in Newport that they met and became engaged) they veered towards the chapel. Mother first took me as a toddler, but after I had caused her much embarrassment she refused to take me again. Apparently, instead of putting a penny in the collection as I was told, I grabbed a handful of loose change to take out of the bag and when the preacher ascended the platform and said, "My text for today is, "Behold the door is open", I piped up load and clear, "No it isn't, it's shut, Betty can see it!" Poor mother! I think she could have died of shame.

When I was old enough to attend Sunday School, I was sent to join in by myself. I started in the babies' class with Miss Mailes. She was a darling. I cannot remember a word of her teaching, but I can still clearly remember the lovely home-made toffee which she brought us all each Sunday. I dare say it helped keep us quiet, but I am sure that was not her principal reason for making it. She was the village postmistress and I am sure she had plenty to do, so how she found time each week to make toffee I do not know.

I progressed to the juniors next, where we all given a small card with a text printed on it which we were supposed to learn by the following Sunday. I had difficulty in remembering these texts for one week, so I regret I cannot now recall any of them. I rather lapsed from Sunday School later on and took to attending Chapel in Ross with my father. Later there were difficulties about getting to Ross and so we attended Hoarwithy Church instead. The Rev. Massey was vicar there then and he was a good friend of my parents.

When I was old enough, Mr. Massey asked if I wanted to be confirmed and my father left it to me to decide whether to become a Baptist or a member of the C of E. I did not fancy being dunked in the water as a Baptist and was by then more familiar with the C of E, so I opted for them. Father declared he did not mind which

I chose as long as I chose something, so I was christened in Hentland church and confirmed the following week in Hoarwithy.

Congregations were much larger in those days, both church and chapel, but I do not think people today are less religious in its broadest sense. Then we all went, partly from habit and partly because there was no other entertainment, or no transport to town on Sundays, so there was nothing much to do and nowhere else to go.

Folk wore their best clothes on Sundays and women all wore hats and gloves to church and it was something of a social occasion as well as a religious one. Work in general stopped on Sundays, and farmers, apart from caring for livestock, did not labour on Sundays. Farm workers had a day of rest and it was only in exceptional crises that hay-making or harvesting were carried out on a Sunday.

My father had strong views about Sunday opening for shops and would go and sit by the river on a Sunday or a Bank Holiday rather than in our own garden in order to escape from importunate shoppers. He did not approve of cinema-going on Sundays either.

Hoarwithy church then had no electricity so the organ was served by a hand-pumped bellows and if the boy or girl doing the pumping was not "on the ball" to make sure there was no lack of wind at the wrong time there could be problems. There was a sexton then who lived in the church house and who cared for the church and grounds. He it was, I suppose, who filled the paraffin lamps and stoked the boiler which warmed the church through a grating in the floor. He also, I remember, released his poultry onto the drive, which was well covered in gravel then and he let the hens pick up all the grains of rice which people threw at weddings and then he would round them up into their pen and rake the gravel level, and behold, all was neat and tidy and the hens had had an extra feed. My father also benefited indirectly because it was probably from our shop that the guests obtained their rice in the first place.

The chapel had one of those organs with foot-pedals and bellows inside it. Would it have been a harmonium, I wonder? It always sounded rather gloomy and depressing I thought.

However, both church and chapel could and did sing lustily and on summer evenings we could enjoy both equally and at the same time if we were in the garden, since we lived between them.

The church had a bell, which the chapel lacked of course. How long is it since that bell was tolled? I know all church bells were silenced during the war years. They were only to be rung if an invasion was imminent. Thank God it never was! I do not know when Hoarwithy bell was silenced. It was not a very cheerful bell in any case – bong – bong – bong!! It was not really a joyful sound, I thought. Our dog was strangely affected by it and would sneak out and sit where he could see the belfry and begin to rock from side to side and lift his muzzle up and howl, a really heart-rending howl. If he caught you looking at him he would stop at once and stalk off in a fury. We could never decide whether the sound caused him agony or ecstasy,

The age-old religious festivals, Christmas, Easter, Harvest, etc. were celebrated by all then as now and both establishments ran Sunday Schools for the children with outings, parties, etc. More of that anon.

Chapter Twenty

Outings

In the twenties and thirties there were not many cars in Hoarwithy. Working people could not afford them and as a result, any outings by charabanc (as couches were called then) were always popular. Sunday Schools, church choirs, the Women's Institute etc. all had summer outings, usually to Barry Island, Porthcawl or Weston-super-Mare. If there were any spare seats on the coach, most organizations were willing to take non-members to make up the numbers.

It took a long time to get anywhere in those days as there were no dual carriageways and no motorways by-passing the towns. The driver going to South Wales had to pass through the city centres of Monmouth, Newport and Cardiff. Therefore there were generally early starts and late returns. On the return journey the coaches usually stopped in Monmouth for fish and chips. There was a convenient "chippy" open till late in the main street.

When I was small the chapel Sunday School asked mother to join them on an outing to Weston-super-Mare, but as she was unable to go, she rather reluctantly agreed for me to go alone, on condition that someone looked after me.

I can remember how disappointed I was when I wanted to paddle in the sea and could not find it as the tide was out and all I found was mud. I became separated from the others and was just beginning to panic when someone swooped down on me and bore me off to a café to have tea. Afterwards I was rather put out to be told to play on the promenade within sight of my teacher (who had her young man with her and probably cursed my presence).

Then came the long ride home. The adults had been plying us with sweets etc. and I disgraced myself by being sick all over Phil Williams' best trousers. (Poor Phil died some years ago, but his widow Norah, is very much part of King's Caple today). He was not pleased, but was very restrained and when I was finally handed over to mother, she was not very pleased either and I had to go across the next day and apologize to Phil's mother for messing up his trousers.

Several times my mother and sometimes I also, joined the outings to Barry and were dropped off and picked up near the home of my grandmother and aunt and spent a day with them instead of continuing to Barry Island.

At Christmas-time both the church and the chapel Sunday Schools gave parties for the children – usually a good feed, presents, Christmas tree etc. Also, there was usually a pantomime in Hereford, at the Kemble Theatre or the Palladium. Both these establishments have long since gone – sunk without trace. Parties came from the villages to enjoy them. Also, villages often had their own pantomimes. I recall seeing "Dick Whittington" at Kings Caple school and the account in Pax of their pantomime last Christmas reminded me of it.

Once, in a year to be remembered, a theatrical troupe came to "Bengatha" (our Hoarwithy Village Hall) and gave nightly performances of real old Victorian dramas. "Maria and the Red Barn" and "The Wicked Squire and the Innocent Village Maiden" type of plays. "Do not darken my doorstep again! Out, out and into the snow" etc. Everyone from far and near came to hear them. We cheered the hero and booed the villain with fervour. How they made a living I do not know. I think the seats were something like a shilling for the front row and 6d and 4d for the rest. I recall father being a bit embarrassed because the manager of the troupe insisted he should have complimentary tickets for the front row in return for advertising their shows.

As I have mentioned before, there were plenty of local entertainments such as dances and whist drives, as well as the outings to the seaside and of course, the cinemas in Ross and Hereford were in their hay-day then, so there was always something going on in rural Herefordshire – more so than now, I think.

CHAPTER TWENTY-ONE

Cats

There were plenty of cats around before the war, some as family pets and some as yard cats. These lived in barns and sheds and their purpose was to keep down the rodent population. All cats were fed on household scraps, bread and milk and sometimes butchers scraps, or offal such as lights (lungs). I suppose there were tins of cat meat around but I do not recollect seeing any.

I can see my mother now, crumbling up bits of bread and putting them in the frying pan to absorb the bacon fat and then pouring on hot water to soften them. She would add any leftovers and scraps and yesterday's milk and then tip the whole panful onto the cats' tin plate up in the yard by the bakehouse. She would bang on the pan and shout, "Puss, puss, puss!" and cats would appear from all directions and fall to.

There were no immunisations for illnesses and I do not think many cats ever got to visit the vet. There were a few Bob Martin's remedies on sale in the shops, but by and large farm cats in particular just took their chances. They lived, propagated, fought, roamed and lived as they pleased and died haphazardly, as chance came their way.

Generally the number of births balanced out the deaths, but if there were too many kittens it was usually possible to find homes for them and if numbers dropped it was not difficult to find someone with kittens to give away.

A farmer's wife in Dewchuch gave my father three kittens once and he put them in a hutch and fed and cared for them and gradually let them out as they grew so that they eventually ran free. He christened them Cuthbert, Clarence and Claud after some music hall act, I believe.

Clarence promptly got run over by one of the bread vans but Cuthbert flourished for some months before meeting his doom. Some small children came rushing in to my mother with the news: "Mrs Russill, the bus has just run over your cat!"

"Oh dear, is it dead?" asked mother,

"Oh yes, very dead", was the answer. So mother decided she had better go and pick up the corpse. She was however unable to find it.

The next thing was a phone call from the owner of Mount Pleasant at the top of the hill. "Mrs Russill, I'm so dreadfully sorry but Chips (his dog) has just come home with a cat and I think it's yours. I can't understand it, he has never killed a cat before. I'm so upset. I've buried it in the garden".

"Don't worry, it was apparently very dead before Chips retrieved it", said mother, "Thanks for burying it".

Claud had better luck and lived to a ripe old age. He had a very distinctive coat, a greyish pepper-coloured fur with a pattern of thin black stripes superimposed on it. Some while later, cats began appearing in Hoarwithy with similar unusual markings, so Claud had obviously passed on his genes.

We had a handsome ginger tom for some time but I think Claud must have ousted him, because he moved down the road to the New Harp and settled in as a pet cat to Mr. Evan Jones, the proprietor.

Father said that when he went to get Mrs Jones' order he would see Ginger comfortably ensconced beside the fire, very contented.

Our dog Terry tolerated cats but obviously considered himself a superior animal. He would ferociously drive off any strange cats who dared to appear.

Mother decided she wanted a house cat and when someone gave her a kitten, she was fearful of Terry's reaction. So she took pains to introduce them and watched like a hawk lest Terry should attack the kitten. She need not have worried. The kitten took to hiding under a low sideboard and darting out and patting at Terry who would in turn, dart after it and crouch down snorting under the sideboard where it had vanished. The kitten would then creep out at the other end and poke Terry from behind and run off again. He seemed to think it was great fun and the two of them would play together. When Terry was tired and lay down by the fire, the kitten would climb across his back and go to sleep too, on top of him.

When I went to Italy to see my son some years ago, he took me out to the farm where he worked and set to work to feed the farm cats. He boiled a big pan of spaghetti, covered it in olive oil and parmesan cheese and doled it out to them. I thought it so odd to see cats all busily eating spaghetti. But I thought, "I suppose this is the Italian equivalent of the English bread and milk". Aren't cats adaptable!

CHAPTER TWENTY-TWO

Wholesalers

When Marks & Spencer opened in Hereford (on the site now occupied by Boots the Chemist) they had a large stock of underwear for ladies in various styles and in all sizes and father happily allowed that he could not compete with them and slowly ran down his sales of underwear and clothing.

Our shop continued to sell sheets, blankets, tablecloths etc. I remember one year there was a sales drive to sell Witney blankets and my father was given a lovely little miniature Witney blanket, about a foot by eighteen inches in size (you young readers can work it out for yourselves in centimetres). I was enchanted by it and coveted it for my doll's bed with great longing and when the sales campaign was eventually over, I acquired it. In the 1990's when the duvet has completely ousted the wool blanket, I was heartened to see a large van in Bath with the slogan "The Witney Horse-Blanket Company". So obviously they are still in existence and have switched to horses. I had seen the blanket factory many years ago, with rows of clotheslines full of newly-made blankets blowing in the wind.

The clothing and drapery side of our shop was supplied by a Cardiff firm whose traveller came to visit my father from time to time and father in turn visited their warehouse on buying trips. I recall going with him once or twice. It was quite a thrill to wander around and look at all the goods on show and listen to the staff extolling their new lines to my father. The only part I not like was the blanket department in the basement. The smell of new wool blankets was over whelming. A dreadful stench!

The warehouse had a metal chute which spiralled all through the building from top floor to basement and as goods were parcelled up they were sent down the chute to the basement to be crated up and dispatched. I thought it was great fun to watch this chute (very like a fair-ground Helter-Skelter) and see the bundles suddenly whiz past and yes I was tempted to try it! But I did not.

After one of these visits a large crate would arrive in Hoarwithy and mother and father would unpack it and check off the contents and then my father would have to work out the cost of each item and mother would sew paper labels onto all the goods with correct price tags. Then the whole lot would be taken up to the back bedroom, which was our drapery room and stacked in boxes on the shelves.

Clothing then was meant to last. People wore things until they wore out. One had a Sunday best outfit and when Easter came around one bought new, if possible and the existing outfit was demoted to second best and eventually became everyday wear. Children's dresses always had big hems, or tucks and each year could be let down an inch or two to keep pace with the child's growth. The local jumble sales (precursors of today's charity shops and car-boot sales) were a source of supply for poorer families then, as now. But today's "throw away" philosophy had no place in village life then.

CHAPTER TWENTY-THREE

Floods and Landslides

We have experienced a fair amount of rain with some quite heavy storms recently, but in total I do not suppose we have exceeded the average for January. So why, oh why have we had such horrible wet, muddy roads with torrents of water pouring down causing floods and landslides?

Part of the answer is obviously the result of modern farming methods: the cultivation of pasture land on hillsides, the filling-in of ponds and neglect of hedges and ditches and so on. but, the other side of the coin is the fact that farmers have to make a living and at the present time life is very difficult for them. One hopes they will manage to follow the guidelines suggested, such as leaving headlands within ploughed fields and ditches each side of hedges where possible and of course, ploughing across and not up and down slopes. (I have heard that grants are available for maintaining hedges properly). Another part of the problem is road maintenance. We always seemed to have a local roadman years ago and I wondered what had happened to him. After some enquiring around I found the name and phone number of the ex-foreman of the Ross area from whom I learned some interesting facts.

Before the amalgamation of Herefordshire and Worcestershire in 1974, the county of Herefordshire employed about 500 roadmen. Each man was responsible for his own "patch" and was expected to keep the roadside ditches clear and to see that all ditches and culverts were cleared out and free from obstruction. He kept the grass swards cut up to the hedges; it was his job to fill in potholes, to keep the roads clear of mud and debris after storms and to clear away snowdrifts in winter.

It was also expected that he would care for the lanes and smaller side-roads as well as the ordinary roads in his area. Wheeled traffic went along lanes then where they certainly would not pass today. When road surfacing was needed, the roadmen from the areas around were called in and they formed a team, working together to get it done.

What a different picture today! There are about 60 roadmen for Herefordshire and Worcestershire, controlled centrally from Spetchley County Hall in Worcester. The old drainage ditches and culverts are not recorded and have in many places silted up; gratings are not cleared and water which is supposed to go down roadside drainage pipes just pours all over the roads as a result. Ponds which were ideal for absorbing surface drainage, have been filled in.

According to my research, there are about 72,000 council-tax paying households in Herefordshire and if 500 roadmen at about £200 per week were to be reinstated, it would cost each household about an extra £64 per annum for their wages. Is this a basis for the new Herefordshire County Council to work on? Why not try to get some action before they take over? It cannot get much worse, can it?

To return to Hoarwithy and district. I found the whereabouts of our last roadman, Mr. Smith, and I went to see him. He is a charming man with many tales to tell. He worked for the Council for 43 years and took early retirement at the age of 62 because he could see redundancy looming after 1974 when the new authority took over.

They sent out teams of time and motion experts which annoyed the roadmen to such an extent that one of them, incensed by being followed everywhere by a man with a stopwatch, grabbed the watch and flung it away.

Mr. Smith was responsible for Hoarwithy, Carey, parts of Bolstone and Little Dewchurch. He told me that the late Charlie Wooding had responsibility for Kings Caple and someone else had the (Rhyd yr Heol) Red Rail end of Hoarwithy.

The water coming down the hill from Little Dewchurch was channelled from the roadside ditches via a large pipe under the road into the field opposite the Phone-box in Hoarwithy and flowed into a very deep concrete pit (over 8 feet deep). It was then drained into the river via a land drain across the meadow. He had, himself, helped to lay the drain. This pit had to be kept clear of mud and debris. The pit is still there, but is choked solid with mud now and the drain in the meadow is fractured.

There was another concrete pit in the gully which drains water down between "40 Steps" and "Wye View". The water comes from the lane at the top of the hill. The late Mr. Johnnie Harris who lived at "40 Steps" some years ago, had a pig, according to Mr. Smith. This pig somehow slipped into the pit and was swept down by the flood waters into another drainage pipe which went under the road and out into the river. Johnnie dashed down to the river, jumped into his boat and paddled furiously after the pig. He managed to catch it and bring it back alive!

We at "Brae Cottage" have a similar pit with a large drainage pipe which goes under our garden and comes out onto the road. When water drains off the fields up above, it flows down a natural gully in "Riverknoll"'s grounds and through our garden. If the pipe gets blocked, or the water is diverted, it all comes down on us and onto "The Biblettes" next door. (Not funny!).

Years ago, our dog, the one who had lived at The Shop, chased a fox down our land drain pipe at "Brae Cottage". The fox, being slim, emerged at the other end, but Terry got stuck, to the distress of my father. Eventually Terry did struggle through. We think there was probably ice in the pipe, as it was mid-winter and frosty. The warmth of his body melted it and allowed him to pass. He was very muddy and cross and hungry when he finally got out.

Mr. Smith knew all the places where blockages might occur and he kept everything clear and running properly. The other roadmen in the county also cared for their own areas. It seems such a shame that things have been so neglected that the roads are in such a state now and all that knowledge has been lost. Local men knew their own area and the public knew who to talk to about local problems.

Post Scriptum

Since this article was written we have heard that Mr. Reginald Smith of Little

Dewchurch, the former Hoarwithy roadman passed away on February 14th. We send our sympathy to his family

Also with the advent of 2001 Herefordshire Council has been reborn and we have a lengthman again, although only part-time and with a bigger area to care for, but it is a start!

CHAPTER TWENTY-FOUR

Christmas Campaign

To plan for Christmas, as any business person will tell you, the planning has to start in advance if the campaign is to be successful. At The Shop, the Christmas campaign would be planned well in advance.

Christmas presents involved a trip to the clothing ware-house to select items such as boxes of handkerchiefs, sets of pillow and bolster cases, all nicely embroidered and tastefully arranged and table-runners and chair backs (out of fashion now). There were many combinations of tea-cosies, egg-cosies, fancy tablecloths and tray-cloths etc. and also things like two dusters and a dish-mop tied together to look like a doll. (I privately thought that sort of gimmick was unfair in the extreme; who wants dish-mops and dusters for Christmas?!). There were gloves and scarves and fancy ties and there were toiletries. The usual soap and talc, much as today, except there were no gels and liquid soaps then; little bottles of scent with flower perfumes were a popular line.

The gifts which really interested me were the sweets and chocolate ones. Cadbury's used to hire rooms in one of Hereford's hotels and send out invitations to all the traders to come and buy. My father took me on several occasions, I think possibly to gauge my reaction to the children's Christmas novelties. I particularly liked some papier maché cats and dogs which were filled with toffees and he bought some of them one year, I remember. An additional bonus on these trips was the gift of a free chocolate bar at the end of the visit.

All the likely ingredients for Christmas cakes, puddings and mincemeat were ordered and a sample case was assembled. There was a square, flat box divided into little square compartments and fronted by glass so that samples of currants, sultanas, raisins, candied peel, cinnamon, cherries etc. could all be shown, with the prices displayed along side. Customers could order in good time to make their cakes and puddings etc. In addition there would be boxes of dates, candied fruit etc. to tempt the customers.

One year my father devoted a week to selling pudding basins. He had a set of them to show at each call. I think there was a tiny one (for a sample pudding to taste) and then there were small, medium, large and family-size ones. He tried to persuade people how useful it would be to have a complete set rather than just one or two basins. He was amused to discover that if he set them out in a row in front of the customer and then tapped them with his pencil they made a tune like a set of handbells.

Most people made their own cakes and puddings then, but he did sell some cakes, Yule Logs etc. ordered from a catalogue which he took to show everyone. I am sure there were other things that came into the scheme of things but I cannot recall them now. I do know it was a carefully planned week-by-week campaign leading to the finale during Christmas week. After it was all over, there would be stocktaking and much calculating to arrive at final figures of how successful his Christmas trading had been.

One year when we had particularly energetic bakehouse staff, the bakers came to him with the suggestion that they make Christmas puddings in the shop. Father was not convinced of the profitability of the scheme, but after thinking it over he gave them the go-ahead and a free hand to take what ingredients they wanted from the shop. They set to with a will, but then discovered their recipe called for brandy or Old Ale or spirits of some sort, so they asked my father to get some. Father asked around and nearly had a fit when he discovered the price of brandy.

Mr. Evan Jones of The Harp came up with a bottle of something (Old Ale, I think) and someone else obtained something else. Father managed a bottle of brandy from somewhere and it all went into the mixture which then had to be boiled. It seemed that the bakehouse was full of steam from cauldrons of boiling Christmas puddings for days. Eventually these puddings were ready to sell. My father set to and worked out the cost of all the ingredients and labour and came to realize that if he charged the correct price no-one would be able to afford them. So he cut his profits down to zero and priced them at the cost of the ingredients. They went very slowly at first but began to pick up and to his relief he did eventually shift them all. Imagine his surprise when customers told him after Christmas that his homemade Christmas puddings were wonderful and what had he put in them? Was he going to make some more? No, thank you, said father; he could not go through all that again!

CHAPTER TWENTY-FIVE

Pests

I mentioned wasps in one of my previous instalments and I must say they really were a problem pre-war. Everyone waged a ceaseless battle against them. They were everywhere in the summer and it was obviously a good idea to destroy their nests if one could find them.

Mr. Garrett who used to live in River Knoll when my parents first came to live here in Brae Cottage, was a tireless tracker-down of wasps' nests. He used cyanide to kill them and my father was always worried to death in case he poisoned himself as well as the wasps. (For those who are unfamiliar with Hoarwithy, River Knoll was where Rev. John Hoskyns lived, above Brae Cottage where I live and now inhabited by the Whites).

People vary a lot in their reactions to wasp stings. Fortunately for my father they had little effect on him, but my mother was allergic to them and reacted very badly if stung and needed medical attention sometimes.

As a very small girl I noticed a hole in the bank one day and poked a stick into it, which resulted in a cloud of angry wasps emerging from it. I yelled in fright and my poor mother coming to the rescue, sustained three stings to her face. Her whole face swelled and turned black and blue and she finished up with one eye completely closed and the other one nearly as bad and was unable to go outdoors for several days. One of the men coming to the door for my father remarked to her, "Good job us knows your husband, or us 'ud think he done it".

Father had the misfortune to be stung by a wasp which crawled up the leg of his trousers one day as he was serving Mrs. Pember (Peter's grandmother). I recall him suddenly erupting into the house from the shop and whipping off his trousers, at which mother and I gaped at him in astonishment. He explained that he had tried to swat it unsuccessfully and by the time he had finished serving Mrs. Pember, it had stung him several times.

During a long hot waspy summer one year a man from Fawley went for a drink at the British Lion and thirstily swallowed down his pint along with a wasp which had just fallen into it. The wasp stung his throat, which swelled rapidly and he was rushed off to hospital hardly able to breath and was saved in the nick of time from death by suffocation.

Flies were also a problem and were combated with sticky fly papers hung from the ceiling and by keeping food etc. covered up.

Rodents were an all-the-year-round pest and war was waged ceaselessly against them.

Rats used to try to settle in the granary, the cellar, the bakery, the outbuildings and by the tracks up through the cavity walls of the house to the attics. They were caught in traps and my father managed to shoot some with his small shot-gun and the cats caught some. Rats are crafty animals and are suspicious of traps and do not offer themselves easily to be shot at. I recall one rat cornered in the cellar, who sat down on a pile of glassware and twiddled his whiskers at us. To shoot at him would have ruined pounds and pounds worth of glass!

Our terrier dog spent all his time looking for rats and would raise the alarm if he could find one. One of their favourite places was behind a sack or corn bin in the granary. I would assist the dog to chivvy the rat around until it bolted for an exit hole which took it onto the sloping roof of the lean-to at the back of the house. From there it would try and leap up to get under the eaves and so to safety in the roof-space but my father would try and shoot it and it would slide down the sloping roof onto the floor below and the dog would rush out and kill it. My mother got roped in for a rat hunt and was told to hold the torch (it was dark at the time) but when the dog caught the rat and tossed it as terriers do, it hit mother on the chest and she yelled and dropped the torch and got shouted at in the heat of battle and so resolved never to have any more to do with rat hunting.

An uncle of mine in London sent father some new "wonder rat-catcher", called (I think) "Rat Sticker". It was a very sticky substance which had to spread onto a sheet of cardboard and placed, with a suitable bait, in the track of the rats. Father tried it out in the yard, away from the cats, but he succeeded only in catching some small birds, which distressed him, so he tried it in the attic where it did catch a couple of rats and also one ginger tom-cat (attracted by the rats, I suppose). Bill tombs, our number one van-driver and father eventually managed to free Ginger by laboriously snipping off most of the fur from his nether quarters. After that "Rat Sticker" was abandoned.

Later another product called "Red Squills" appeared on the market. This was a powder that had to be mixed with lard or something similar and put down in dollops for the rodents to eat. It was supposed to be harmless to all other animals. So once again, father went up to the attic and put down spoonfuls of this stuff in all likely places. He did it by torch-light and was vaguely aware of a slight noise, but it was not until he had finished that he realized that our grey cat had been following and had eaten it all as fast as he spread it. It did not seem to have any adverse effect on the cat, so it probably was harmless to other animals.

Another time father decided to lay down a concrete floor in one of the outbuildings where he suspected rats were tunnelling under the earth. Next day the still damp concrete was full of holes, so he blocked them all up except one and ran a hose from the car exhaust down that one in the hopes of gassing a few rats. It stopped that means of entry, but I expect they soon found a way around it.

In the house one could hear mice running around in the space between the bedroom floor and the downstairs ceiling. They got in via the granary which abutted onto the house, so we kept a baited mouse-trap under there, accessed via a loose floor board. If the dog heard the trap snap he would rush upstairs and wait impatiently for someone to remove the floorboard so that he could remove the mouse.

The yard cats kept the mice under control outside the house and they caught the odd rat or two.

I do not think rabbits bothered us too much, but to the farmers they were a very real pest, kept down to some extent by professional rabbit-catchers. One often saw these catchers with sticks of rabbit carcasses going to market. Many people ate rabbits as a regular part of their diet, but of course the advent of myxomatosis killed that off.

Many country people kept ferrets and did a bit of rabbiting in their spare time, or else set out snares for rabbits.

Gamekeepers have always waged war on any pests which have threatened their game, but today I should think mink and perhaps magpies are the main culprits.

CHAPTER TWENTY-SIX

Telephones

We all have phones these days, do we not? Anyone who does not, is very much the odd man out.

In my childhood the majority of cottages did not have phones and as I have mentioned before, those people who did have phones were used to the idea of their neighbours coming to them in an emergency.

It was necessary for us to have a phone at the shop, for business purposes and ours was installed in the late twenties (I think). Our number was Carey 5 and our local exchange was in Carey Post Office. The Post Office was in Pear Tree Farm, adjacent to the Cottage of Content (or the Miners' Arms as it was then).

The Terry family ran the farm and the Post Office. Mrs Terry and latterly her daughter Violet, did most of the telephone work. It was the type of exchange where a handle was turned vigorously (in order to make the phone ring at the other end?) after inserting a wire into a plughole on the switchboard to connect the caller to the number he wanted. The switchboard was opened at 7am and closed at 10pm, so there were no night calls.

I can still remember my very first, all by myself telephone call! It was one Saturday afternoon. Violet Terry belonged to Hoarwithy Tennis Club and the club was playing an away match, to which my father was driving the team. He had been delayed by work and came dashing into the house to change and asked me to phone Violet to say he would be collecting her in about ten minutes.

I felt very important and cautiously picked up the ear-piece and prepared to say this to Violet, when she answered. I was totally unprepared for the voice which said, "Number, please?" I did not know what to do. Did this voice want my number or Violet's number? What was Violet's number anyway? I was struck dumb! "Who's calling?" asked the voice,

"Me", I said. Violet probably guessed it was me and asked kindly,

"Is that you Betty?", to which I gasped out,

"Yes" and then went on to deliver my message. Phew! Telephones were not to be treated lightly.

To phone out of the district it was necessary to ask for "trunks", which often meant delays and sometimes failure to get through at all. If there was a backlog of callers for a trunk line, the operator would say, "I'll phone back to you when I get a line". I do not remember when the old Carey Exchange tuned into a brick "hut" on the Kings Caple side of the bridge and operators faded away and S.T.D. came in. These days it is easier to talk to relatives in Canada or Australia than it was in those days to call Ross.

The party-line was common, particularly in the post-war years and was not too popular if one party was an eavesdropper or had teenagers who gossiped.

Phone boxes, of course, have always been popular, but today they are used mostly by people who are away from home. In the past they were used by people who did not have phones. I recall years ago my mother-in-law going up to the corner phone box to ring my husband's brother and dialling, putting in the money and as soon as the call was answered saying, "Hello Bill, this is Mum", only to hear a supercilious voice say, "Madam, my name is not Bill, I haven't got a Mum and you have the wrong number!" and she was promptly cut off. How is that for a put down.?

To be connected to a phone it was necessary to live near a phone line and even today I suspect it is necessary to pay to have the lines brought near to you.

When father was a member of the old Ross and Whitchurch Rural District Council, the council was asked to pay for a phone box to be situated in a lonely valley, a long way from the nearest phone lines. There was a farm and two or three cottages at the head of the valley and the residents pleaded, "What do we do if there is a medical crisis or some catastrophe?". So after some grumbling and expense, the council paid for the phone box. As soon as it was installed and there was a line in place, the farm and one of the cottages asked for their own phones which they could then afford.

When the meter man came to empty the collecting box in the phone booth, he found a ram tied up inside. The farmer came and removed it and explained it was a handy place to put him whilst waiting to move him to another field. The collecting box when opened contained about 2 1/2d and some foreign coin. Can you blame the council for feeling it had been conned?

CHAPTER TWENTY-SEVEN

Pigs and Horses

PIGS: "Bacon from the supermarket does not taste like bacon used to, does it?". Pre-war, most farmers and cottagers kept a pig or two for home consumption and most of us at some time or other were able to taste some locally grown bacon, pork or sausages. Even if we did not keep a pig, a present from a friend or neighbour would occasionally come our way. In any case, the bacon we sold in the shop tasted like bacon.

If you walk around as you walk through the village you will notice that many cottages still have traces of an old pigsty. The pig would be fed on pig-meal augmented by household peelings and scraps and any surplus from the vegetable garden.

When the great day came that the pig was slaughtered, it was all hands on deck to deal with the joints, offal and lard etc. I recall going with a school friend to Auntie somebody to request "Some rosemary for the lard, please". Rosemary finely chopped, gave the lard a lovely flavour. Lard, like beef-dripping was used for sandwiches sometimes and was very tasty.

At garden-fêtes, "bowling for a pig" was quite a star attraction and a good money-raiser. A local farmer would be cajoled into donating a piglet and the organisers would hire a bowling alley and charge say, sixpence (21/2p) a go. The person with the highest score at the end of the day would win the pig, which would be on display in a makeshift pen beside the bowling alley. This would sometimes generate fierce rivalry between the contestants who would come back time and again for another go if somebody else chalked up a higher score than the previous one.

I do not know what the rules were then for slaughtering pigs; no doubt many farmers were able to slaughter their own. I know many cottagers employed a professional slaughterman to do it for them. The "pigsticker" was an itinerant who travelled as he was needed. I sat next to one on the bus one day. He carried the tools of his trade in a sack beside him. I remember thinking what a mild-mannered, pleasant little man he seemed and wondering how he could bring himself to earn a living killing pigs.

Cart-Horses

I suppose most people associate them with farm work before the war, but they worked at other things as well. A horse would be used to tramp round and round a cider the cider-mill to squash the apples. Most farms made their own cider and gave it to the men at harvest and at haymaking time. (It was pretty potent stuff too!). I think the rationing of sugar and the decline in the number of horses killed that. Breweries used horse-drawn drays and some still do, I believe. The use which sticks in my mind is horse-drawn timber-wagons. Forestry has seen enormous changes over the years. It seems to be largely conifers which are grown and felled now and all is mechanised to the extreme.

Timber felling used to be done by axes, or big two-handed cross-cut saws. (The chainsaw had not been invented then.). The tree trunks were hauled out of the woods by horses and then loaded onto a timber-carriage to be taken away. Many went to their destination by rail and since our local station was Ballingham I saw them go past.

Timber wagons always travelled in pairs. There were three carthorses for each wagon and a carter and a waggoner with each. When they came to a hill, the horses from the second wagon would be unhitched and added to the three on the first wagon. Then the whole team would strain and pull and work up momentum to get the wagon going at a pace to rush up the hill and get to the top. The load would usually consist of one big oak or elm tree-trunk or sometimes two or three smaller ones. After a breather, the team would go down and bring up the second wagon.

It was going downhill that really called for skilful handling. The carter would put a brake on the back wheels, a sort of metal "shoe" which stopped the wheels from turning. He would steer the left side well into the bank to slow it down. His most experienced horse would be in the shafts next to the wagon and he would lean back and push hard as they went down to prevent the wagon getting out of control. It was wonderful to watch the great horse straining every muscle to hold back the weight as they slid down the hill with the carter steering it so skilfully.

From Hoarwithy to Ballingham there was first of all the hill up past the Haynes Farm and then following that the very steep Carey pitch going down to a right-angled bend at the "Cottage of Content" and then once more a steep hill up past the Rock Farm with a sharp bend at the top.

What a difficult and time-consuming job it was in those days to get timber from A to B! But what a thrilling sight to see those wonderful horses! It seems so sad they have gone from the rural scene. Progress, I suppose!

CHAPTER TWENTY-EIGHT

Brae Cottage

Towards the end of the thirties an event occurred which surprised my parents. A lady, Miss Anderson by name, who lived at Brae Cottage was suddenly obliged to sell the cottage to go and care for a sick relative and not liking the idea of all the hassle involved with estate agents etc. she came and offered to sell the cottage to the Russills (my parents). She pointed out that they could let it and that when they wished to retire it would be there for them.

My parents decided to accept her offer and accordingly the cottage was let to an elderly lady, the mother of a local man for seven and sixpence (371/2p) a week. She was an astute old lady, who promptly sublet one bedroom and a sitting-room to another old lady for five shillings (25p) a week.

When they left it, my father used the cottage for various relatives during the war years and also let it at one stage to a baker from Birmingham whom he employed in the bakery.

Pre-war the big munitions factory at Rotherwas was slowly drawing in workers from all over the county and the labour shortage which resulted meant that he could no longer replace staff when they left by employing local people. At about this time the youngster from the bakery went to Rotherwas and father had to do some of the bakery work himself and then when old Walter Newport left, he took on this young man from Birmingham. He seemed a quiet competent baker and was happy to live at Brae Cottage, so it was a shock when the police turned up one day and drove him off to Birmingham on burglary charges.

The police told my father that the man was a known professional burglar and that he had come to Hoarwithy so that he could live a legitimate baker's life during the week and then go to Birmingham at the weekends "to visit relatives", but actually to rob the citizens of Birmingham and sell the loot and return to the life of an innocent baker for the following week. Naturally father wondered if he had stolen anything from us, but he was assured that the man was too clever to draw attention to himself by committing any crimes here.

Eventually, when the war in Europe ended, my parents moved here themselves. My father was worn out with running the business, doing air-raid warden's work etc. non stop for five years. He had an eye condition and had been to the Victoria Eye Hospital in Hereford a couple of times and was told if he did not stop work he would go blind, so they sold up and came here and he did rest and his health improved after a few months.

Father set to work to improve Brae Cottage, constructing a water-tank, as I have previously mentioned. He wanted to install a bath as there was no bathroom here then, only two rooms upstairs and two down and a corrugated-iron lean-to at the side of the house which was used as a general storeroom.

At that time there was an acute shortage of metal (I suppose it all went for making tanks, guns and planes) so that it was necessary to get a permit for the purchase of a metal bath (plastics were then in the future). My father accordingly obtained the requisite form and filled it in. In answer to the question, "Why do you require the article?", he replied, "Live too far from river"! In time he was able to order his bath and eventually it arrived.

It was summertime and my parents were, as they say, "taking tea on the terrace" with a visiting vicar and his wife from London. Mother's version of events was that a strange young man appeared on the steps and said, "Your bath has come, but I'm on my own, so you must come and help me unload it". The vicar and my father accordingly went to help and the three of them laboriously heaved it all the way up to the terrace. (Anyone who knows Brae Cottage will realize that this was no mean feat!!).

Eventually father plumbed in the bath in the lean-to, where when covered over when not in use it made an extra table.

A few years after the war, when builders and building materials were once more available, a major enlargement and alterations programme was undertaken and a proper upstairs bathroom was installed and the house modernised. When, years later in the mid 1980's my husband retired and we came here to live, we in our turn updated the cottage yet again. I do not think Miss Anderson, were she to come alive today, would recognize it.

I suspect that many of the cottages in the area have had similar changes, extensions and modernisations carried out. Progress? Yes!

CHAPTER TWENTY-NINE

Tales of Hoarwithy People

Marret Cottage near my home has seen some changes. When I first was aware of it, there was an elderly couple living there, who I believe, had retired there from the tropics. Richards, I think, was their name. He had a snowy white beard and wore a red cummerbund and reminded me vaguely of Father Christmas. They felt the cold very badly and were delighted when father suggested a Valour heater and they eventually bought two from him. Father said their living room was like an oven. It was so hot with a coal fire and two paraffin heaters all going full blast. The old gentleman used to look out for me coming home from Ballingham School and ask me to post a letter for him, which I was quite happy to do and was overjoyed that he usually gave me some pennies or a threepenny-piece.

The village builder Mr.James, was the next person I remember living at Marret Cottage. He, as was his custom, enlarged and improved the place and painted all the woodwork a pale sky-blue and the walls a pale pinkish shade. I suppose he liked those colours as he always seemed to use them on every house he "improved".

I next remember the Landsfields. They met, I believe, at the guest house and each believing the other had private means, they married. They were middle aged and did not settle down too well. In fact they had some thundering quarrels. She, if rumour was to be believed, nagged him shamefully and was not popular with the village because she was fanatical about animal welfare and told other people how to care for their animals. A Miss Lewis who lived nearer the centre of the village had a pony and trap and obviously knew how to care for her pony was not amused to have Mrs Landsfield buying bread from the shop and feeding it to the pony because "it was starving!".

The Landsfields had a poor old dog who was very ill with a heart condition and eventually it died. She had a large wooden box made especially as a coffin and buried the dog in the garden. A workman subsequently unearthed it long after Mrs Landsfield was gone. He thought it was a treasure chest, but the stench when he opened it nearly flattened him.

The two guest houses, Upper Orchard and The Aspens, were under one management pre-war. I think it was a Mr Andrew Mailes and family who owned it. I can remember Bertie, a little man with a Clarke Gable moustache and a worried air and his sister Grace Mailes, who actually did most of the work and I think it was after the Mailes family retired that it was split into two separate establishments.

The Mailes took in holiday-makers, but the bulk of their trade seemed to be elderly retired people who lived there permanently. Miss Bolton is the only lady I clearly remember. She was a dignified Edwardian lady who was always well dressed with hat, gloves and parasol.

Another guest was Mr Uniack, a portly gentleman, who was one of the leading lights in building Bengatha, the Village Hall. I think Mr Uniack was Australian, but I am not sure. He was a leading light in many village affairs for a time and supported village organizations and like many others before him, he tried to "organize the natives" who stubbornly refused to be organized. Herefordians do not like being hustled.

Another guest whom I remember was Mr Satchell. He was an elderly man and very spruce and upright, ex-army, I imagine. He talked to himself and would march briskly around the village, striding along with his head up. My mother came home from Hereford on the bus with him one day and was most intrigued to hear him suddenly burst into peals of laughter and remark "Too much fish!". It was obviously some episode involving fish which he was remembering, but what? We thought of that whenever we saw him.

After war broke out the guesthouses received various people fleeing from the bombing in London, but I can only remember a Jewish gentleman called Mr. Israel.

CHAPTER THIRTY

More Hoarwithy People

I have written about how life was pre-war, but very little about the people who actually lived here then. There were many interesting and eccentric characters around and plenty of events to gossip about.

At the Red Rail (Rhyd yr Heol yn cymraeg!) end there was Sam Romney and his son, Reg Romney who mended all the boots and shoes in Hoarwithy. Sam sang in the church choir on Sundays and unfortunately had a very load and raucous voice and caused some pain to those of the congregation who were in the least musically inclined. My father appealed to the Rev. Massey, but he reminded him that the Bible exhorted Christians to praise the Lord with a loud voice and he could not do anything about it.

Does anyone remember Colin Price? He was a very deaf painter and decorator who lived in half of Lavender Cottage (also Red Rail/Rhyd yr Heol). He came to paint the exterior of the shop and asked mother for some rags for his paint brushes and she was most amused to hear him saying, "A nice piece of cloth" about some rayon undergarment which she had given him – he put it away as being too good to use as a paint rag. She wondered what he did use it for. He talked to himself most of the time and was obviously unaware that he was audible to everyone around him.

Another painter lived in the cottage at Mount Pleasant. I think he was before Colin Price's time. His wife used to button-hole my mother to weep on her shoulder and tell her the sad story of how she adopted a baby because she had none of her own and this baby grew up to be a beautiful little girl with blonde curls and was loving and adored by all and then the parents appeared one day out of the blue and told her the adoption had never been legalised and took the little girl away and she never saw her again.

Along the Carey road in Hoarwithy was old Sally Griffiths. She had formerly lived in the top flat of Tarrystones, but took to throwing her rubbish out of the window, to the annoyance of the gentleman living below. He was a builder called Mr James, who specialized in buying a house, moving in and doing it up and moving on to another one. He was currently in Tarrystones. He solved the problem of Sally Griffiths by building a little two-roomed bungalow next to The Holt on the Carey road, down below Tarrystones.

My mother used to visit Sally with gifts of tea, sugar etc. from time to time. I can remember her telling mother that the chimney was smoking so she was going to walk to London to ask the chimneysweep who had attended her employers' house there to come and sweep hers. I was impressed with the enormous walk and wondered how she would do it. I can see her now in a bonnet and shawl, looking like the pictures of Queen Victoria. I think it could not have been long after that when she was taken to an old persons' home. A tramp subsequently broke into the bungalow and accidentally set fire to it. Since Sally had saved scraps of paper, string, old newspapers etc. for years, it burnt furiously and was soon reduced to rubble and all trace of it was soon obliterated.

Tom Bond the saddler, who lived and worked in his little shack at the bottom of River Knoll drive, has already appeared in Pax, but he certainly deserves another mention. Half of his shack was his workshop and the other half was his home. He had a kitchen-range, an armchair and a bunk bed. He often left the door open and it always looked so warm and cosy to see the fire burning away and Tom in his armchair. He took pity on a local tramp called Bill Guy and took him in as a lodger for a time. I wondered how they managed their sleeping arrangements. I suppose the lodger slept in the armchair.

A Mrs. Watkins lived at The Salmons and sold milk. We got our milk from her until she gave up. Her brother (I think that was where he fitted in) kept the cows and as he had not much grazing for them, he often took them along the road to graze on the grass verges. He would go with them and move them to one side to allow vehicles to pass.

The milk supply passed to Dolly and Jim Oldis who lived at The Mill before Carol Probert took it on. Dolly had a small herd of cows which she cared for with love and attention and they produced the milk which their foster-son, Percy Hill delivered around the village in a Jeep. Dolly was a large lady, usually dressed in Wellingtons and an overall and was a great personality who knew everyone and everything that went on in the village, although she seldom left The Mill, but very little escaped her attention.

CHAPTER THIRTY-ONE

The New Harp

The village Inn is traditionally supposed to be the centre of village life and thanks to the hard work of successive landlords it still is in Hoarwithy. The character of the village inns has changed and adapted over time, but their welcome remains.

When I was small, women were not welcome, beer was much cheaper and the clients tended to be from homes within walking or cycling distance. Very little food was served and drinking and talking were the main concerns. I cannot speak from personal knowledge, as I did not enter any of the locals when I was young.

In Hoarwithy, the space outside The Harp was the scene of various activities central to the village.

At times of parliamentary elections the would-be M.P.'s would tour the villages and harangue the locals, who were by no means backward in coming forward with their questions and comments. I can recall some gentlemen standing on a farm cart to talk to us all and a farmer in the crowd complaining about the government's policy on Herefordshire bulls. What his grievance was, I cannot remember, but the politician could not give him a straight answer (do they ever?) and the farmer caused the poor man some embarrassment because he would not let it rest, but kept coming back to it, with the support of the crowd.

On one occasion a mobile caravan parked outside The Harp to give us all a demonstration of some revolutionary new washing powder. (Rinso or Persil maybe?). It sounded too good to be true, as at that time Sunlight Soap was still widely used for washing clothes and the idea of a powder in hot water to do the job instead of rubbing with a bar of soap, was quite new. I believe the lady encouraged us to bring her our dirty clothes and she would show us how it was done, but the ladies of the village were not that keen to have their dirty linen washed in public.

Then in the autumn the blackberry lorry would go the rounds of all the villages to buy blackberries. A notice would be nailed to the chestnut tree outside The Harp, stating the times the buyer hoped to arrive at each village and the current price per pound for blackberries. People would appear with baskets, buckets or even tin foot-baths and the lorry would arrive and the buyer would weigh the fruit and pay out the money and off he would go till next week.

I thought at the time that the blackberries went to make blackberry jam, but learned years later that it was for dyeing that they were needed. When the synthetic aniline dyes came on the market, the blackberries were no longer needed and the practice was dropped. However, the blackberry harvest did earn many people some welcome extra cash in those days.

The fox hunt then, as now, met at either such places as Aramstone or Caradoc, or more frequently then, in front of The Harp. It was a pleasure to see all the hounds and horses, the red coats and all the ritual of a hunt getting under way. I cannot remember feeling any moral objection then to fox hunting and whatever your feelings on the subject, it is still quite a show to look at, even if one does not approve of hunting.

On Remembrance Sunday, all the members of the local British Legion would turn up for church parade. They would assemble and march into church and afterwards, back to The Harp for "Dismiss" and in for a drink and a yarn. The church was full of ex-service men then, most of them (like my father) long gone.

My childhood memory is of an overpowering smell of mothballs (from Sunday suits) and a gentle clinking of medals. I am sure the landlord of those days did well from the sale of beer.

The Church Army sent a caravan with two Army Sisters to Hoarwithy once a year. I am not sure why. Both churches and chapels held religious rallies around the district from time to time. I vaguely remember a marquee on occasions as well and fervent hymn singing etc. so I expect it was in connection with that.

The Sisters did not park outside The Harp. Avoiding the demon drink, I suppose. But they did the next best thing and parked in the yard of The Mill opposite. I fear the only thing I remember about them is that our terrier dog (he of the ratting fame) took a dislike to them and disgraced himself by biting one of them. I think possibly it was not, as some local wag put it about, that Terry was a secret Roman Catholic, but it was more to do with the fact that Mrs Oldis who lived at The Mill was a great favourite with him and he obviously thought the Sister was trespassing.

Sometimes men would be a nuisance in one village public house and would transfer their allegiance to an adjacent one, landlords could tell them they were unwelcome and it was through that means that The Harp acquired a farmer from Little Dewchurch. He was a bit of a trouble-maker I believe, but he did come to The Harp for a while. He always came by horse, accompanied by a dog. After closing time he would clamber aboard the horse (a big cart-horse) and go galloping past our shop with a great clatter of hooves and barking from the dog. The horse obviously was wanting to get back to the stable and galloping hard.

In the summer season the campers from Birmingham, who lodged in the field by The British Lion, often came to The Harp in the evenings and would stagger off to bed singing the latest songs. We would hear "Red Sails in the Sunset" etc. gradually fading away as they climbed the hill across the river.

Mr. Evan Jones and his wife ran The Harp for many years and were popular in the village in the forties. The beer came from Ross – The Alton Court Brewery where Somerfield is now situated. It was bought out and closed down long ago.

I think that is enough about The Harp for now and let us be thankful that we still have our village inns and long may they flourish.

CHAPTER THIRTY-TWO

More Recollections

The large corrugated-iron barn on Ballingham road, which was demolished fairly recently, was originally the home for agricultural machines belonging to a Mrs Lewis who lived further along the road. She was a widow, a tiny lady, all in black when I first became aware of her and she carried on her husband's business. I found it enthralling to watch her thrashing machine at work. It was powered by a steam engine, via a moving belt and it clanked and clattered away in clouds of dust and steam, the men tossing the sheaves at the top and collecting the grain and straw which emerged. It seemed to me to be so much more exciting than watching a combine-harvester tearing around a present day field. (It could not be anything to do with being older could it?).

That barn was always red in colour and was only painted black some years post-war, so the older people will still think of the RED BARN as a village landmark.

Mrs Lewis had two daughters who continued living in the village after her death.

Gert, the one daughter, married a Mr Fred Eaves and lived at Underhill. She faithfully played the church organ in Hoarwithy for years. Mr Eaves was the village insurance agent and went around collecting the weekly contributions for, I think, the Prudential. You could say the wheel has come full circle now with Mr David Gibbs living there. (Pax readers will know that he is in insurance.).

Mrs Lewis' other daughter lived at home and was the village dressmaker. I can well remember the lovely tweed jacket she made for me long ago. She was the owner of the pony and trap. The pony was called Zoe and was the cause of the rumpus with Mrs Landsfield, who would persist in feeding it bread.

No account of Hoarwithy would be complete without mentioning The Mill. When I was small Mr and Mrs Dance lived there with their adopted son Jim Oldis. He was some relative of theirs and they took him in because they had no children of their own. When I first knew him he was a very handsome and dashing young man with flashing dark eyes and lovely curly black hair and the object of pursuit by the village maidens of the day. The mill was working in those days, but I do not think it produced large amounts of flour. I know my father always got his bread flour from Hereford Flour Mills, which alas, is no more today.

Jim Oldis married a Dewchurch girl called Dolly and he went to live at The Weaven Farm, but returned to The Mill to take over when Mr Dance died. Jim and Dolly and the cows settled there and ran the dairy and milk round from there for years. The Mill ceased to function and Jim took on various jobs, local coal merchant, taxi service etc. After Dolly died and Jim retired, he sold out to his cousin Carol Probert who continues to do good business, albeit of the bed and breakfast variety.

The actual mill is now a private house, though the owner assured me that the wheel is still there.

Old Mrs Dance lived on at The Mill to become a centenarian. She was a very interesting old lady and I enjoyed talking to her. I have mentioned her in previous episodes. She and Dolly did not always see eye to eye, not surprising as they were both strong-minded characters with very positive ideas and opinions. I recall a long-running feud over the correct accompaniments for roast turkey. One maintained it was bread sauce and the other cranberry or red currant jelly. I am not sure exactly, but I know they each sought opinions from other people to support their own viewpoint. My poor mother tried to be diplomatic and not offend either of them.

This led me to the conclusion that maybe some people enjoy a good quarrel to break the monotony of their lives.

CHAPTER THIRTY-THREE

The Tickles

The Tickles lived in a pleasant house, opposite Ballingham Rectory in the Carey area. He had worked in the colonies and she was from Australia. He was a firm believer in the British Empire and stood for the then fashionable idea that it was the duty and obligation of all the colonials to deal firmly and honestly with the "natives" and always to look after those not as fortunate in life as themselves. They were a couple who helped many people in Ballingham, Little Dewchurch and Carey in an unobtrusive way and I am sure many of those people were very thankful.

They were very active supporters of the local schools, i.e. Ballingham and Little Dewchurch. When I was a pupil of Ballingham School we were all invited to their house on Empire Day (May 14th, I think!). We sang carefully rehearsed patriotic songs, "Land of Hope and Glory", Hearts of Oak", etc. and of course the National Anthem (all the verses!). Then Mr Tickle made a speech all about the Glorious British Empire (pronounced "Empah"!) and how we should feel proud to be citizens of it etc. and then Mrs Tickle would give us all glasses of lemonade, slices of fruit cake, oranges etc.

Every child was given a very nice medal with the head of the Prince of Wales on one side and something about the Empire on the other. (The late Duke of Winsor was Prince of Wales then). Each year we got a bar to stick onto the medal ribbon and by the time each child left school it was quite an impressive sight. In those far off days it seemed to be always a lovely sunny day and we enjoyed the walk across the fields to the Tickles' house and their lawns seemed to be always green and well tended and we were allowed to play there before going home.

The only flaw in the day was that Mr Tickle was profoundly deaf and used an ear trumpet to hear us and of course it made talking to him very difficult. We were mostly too much in awe of him to attempt to speak anyway.

He was interested in country pursuits and he had a very old decrepit Spaniel dog. The story goes that Mr Tickle was walking on the riverbank one day with his old dog when he met a neighbour and stopped to pass the time of day. The neighbour had heard that Mrs Tickle was unwell, so naturally he asked, "How is the wife?" but unfortunately he was bending over to pat the dog at the time and old Mr Tickle, thinking he was referring to the dog, replied, "Oh, the old bitch wants shooting". This episode went the rounds of all the local villages in no time! In passing I might add that old or injured animals were mostly shot in those days – it being the most humane way of putting them down as vets were too distant and expensive.

My father used to call at the Tickle home once a week for the grocery order. He mostly saw their cook, but if the old gentleman had a query or complaint he would ask for father to come and see him. He employed a butler called Sam, a smart, self-confident young man who delighted in conducting father into the presence and then stationing himself behind Mr Tickle, from whence he could make ribald comments in the hope of disconcerting my father. However Sam had a dreadful shock one day when he was sued for Breach of Promise by a determined and vengeful young lady. Father heard all about it and told us.

Now Sam was apparently something of a ladies' man, but was usually astute enough to steer clear of any commitments, but this time he found himself firmly committed to wed the lady and when he tried to break it off she sued him and he had to go to court, where the judge gave him a very rough time and awarded damages of £20 against him. This would be the equivalent of about six months wages I expect, if not more, by today's standards.

Sam had had to confess to Mr Tickle and ask for the day off to go to court and was very much afraid he would be dismissed, as he knew Mr Tickle would not countenance such behaviour. When he returned Mr Tickle called him into his study and gave him an absolutely blistering reprimand and called him the lowest of the low etc., etc. and finally handed him an envelope and told him to get out and that if he ever did such a thing again he would be instantly dismissed and "Don't be such a damn fool ever again!" When Sam had recovered and realized that he had not been dismissed, he opened the envelope and found a cheque for £20! I think this gives you an idea of the calibre of Mr Tickle.

He died in the early 1940's and Mrs Tickle, whose eyesight was failing by then, decided to return to Australia and escape the war in Britain. Unfortunately the poor old lady arrived in Australia just in time to be bombed by the Japanese.

CHAPTER THIRTY-FOUR

The Scudamores

This is mostly about the Scudamores. They are a very old family whose name crops up again and again in the history of our benefice. Lady Scudamore revived the Pax Cakes tradition. It had been started years previously by another lady, so that Lady Scudamore gave the money for cakes and cider for the poor which was the origin of our Pax Cake tradition. Look at the memorials in our churches and the name appears quite often.

My first memory of the Scudamores is of a middle-aged couple farming at Ruxton. They had a son and two daughters. The son was called Geoffrey and he was a rather wild young man. He was sent to Canada to relatives and came back sporting some brightly coloured cowboy shirts, quite a novelty then and a topic of conversation amongst us all. He had a gift for getting into trouble and was the object of much gossip (no doubt highly exaggerated). He drove his car off the road one night and it crashed through the hedge and turned over and came to rest on the river bank where it was found the following morning, upside down with him fast asleep inside it. He subsequently married and lived on the Ballingham road for a while. I can remember his son Michael in his pram outside their house. Then he moved away and the next I remember hearing was that he joined the R.A.F. at the outbreak of war and was shot down over Germany and spent the rest of the war as a P.O.W.. He came home safely when the war ended and settled down.

His son Michael grew to be a jockey and all of Hoarwithy went wild when he won The Grand National on a horse called Oxo. Unfortunately he suffered a bad fall not long afterwards and had to retire from racing, but I am sure you all know he trained and bred racehorses at Prothither Farm at Bromley for many years and has only recently sold the farm and retired to help his equally famous son Peter. Peter was champion jockey a few years ago and now he too has retired and gone in for breeding and training horses.

There was another Scadamore around in the twenties and thirties – Johnnie Scudamore who was Clerk to the Parish Council. I do not know if he had been a jockey in his youth. He was small and very bandy and rode a motorcycle very cautiously. He held it at arms' length as thought it were a horse of whose temper he was uncertain, so I expect he too had raced horses in his youth.

The Scudamore parents who lived at Ruxton had a very large and ferocious Alsatian dog which was rumoured to attack strangers coming to the house. When my father called to see Mrs Scudamore to take the grocery order, he would always wait outside the door in the courtyard wall if Simon (as the dog was called) was loose and Mrs Scudamore would come out and take the dog inside and shut him up and then call to father to come in. One day however, just as father approached the door Mr

Scudamore emerged. He wished father "Good day" and went off and as all was quiet father assumed Simon was shut in the house, so he pushed the door open and was immediately knocked flat by Simon who was trying to follow his master. My father prepared to defend himself from attack, but nothing happened and when he looked around Simon was running away with his tail between his legs, scared stiff of father. When he got inside he asked Mrs Scudamore about Simon and she explained, "He's a real softie and would not hurt anyone, but we put it around that he's savage and a wonderful guard dog who protects the farm and since we have had him we have been free of petty pilfering which has been plaguing us, but please Mr Russill don't give the game away".

Thereafter when Simon rushed out and barked at him, father had only to shout "Lie down" and Simon crept away.

Unfortunately Simon came to untimely end when he chased a rabbit up the railway tunnel at Fawley and met a train coming the other way.

Prothither Farm where Michael Scudamore lived was inhabited by the Sherrat family when I was small. Mr Sherrat, a quiet, kindly man used to take the milk-churns from the farm to Ballingham station every day and as he passed the shop, it was arranged between him and father that he took me as well when I first started school. I enjoyed riding in the pony trap and I think he enjoyed the company. It was a big help to me as I only had to walk from the station to school.

Mrs Sherrat, an ardent chapel goer, was the type who watched the pennies very carefully all week and made a profit wherever she could and when she got to hear of the arrangement, presented father with a bill for transporting me to the station, which father promptly countered by presenting her with a bill for transporting her groceries. Stalemate. So she dropped the idea. She had two daughters and she brought them up to think highly of themselves.

The younger one (my age) was, in my eyes, a proper little goody-two-shoes and I must have been really horrible to her when she came to Hereford school later on and I was asked to look after her because she did not know anyone else there. Mrs Sherrat was supposed to have told the school doctor, "My daughter is different from other children!" meaning she was a good well-behaved girl who never did any wrong, but the school doctor replied, "Oh, poor little thing. Whatever is the matter with her?" Which did not please Mrs Sherrat.

CHAPTER THIRTY-FIVE

Red Rail: (Rhyd yr Heol)

The second house, at the bottom of Sheppon Hill, was the wheelwright's. I can see him now, busy making a wagon wheel. I think it was the house now occupied by the lady who breeds and shows Pekingese dogs. If you call there you are likely to be engulfed in a tidal wave of vigorously yapping Pekes of all colours.

Nearer the centre of the village there were two families in adjoining cottages each of whom had an assortment of teenagers. The daughter of one family had a little girl, allegedly fathered by one of the sons next door and the two old ladies enjoyed a good row every now and then (I suspect it was sheer boredom, as life must have been dull in those days with no TV or radio and little money for going out). The granny of the little girl would say, "Go and knock on next door and when she answers say, "Hullo Granny"". Of course the other lady would rise to the bait and say, "I'm not your Granny!" etc., etc. and the rest of the day would be spent in them screeching insults at each other.

My mother had a friend living near them and when it got too fortissimo she would come along to see mother for a break. She had several children and I was always happy to play with the two older ones who were in my age group. I missed them when the family moved away.

On one of my birthdays when those two came to tea with me, my father had made and iced a surprise birthday cake, but owing to my grandfather's sudden death, he had to make an urgent trip to London and simply did not have time to decorate it, so he put three sugar mice from the shop onto the top of the cake and said to mother, "Tell her it's the three blind mice". My two friends from Red Rail and I had a lovely party and the cake was a great success. As Douglas, the little boy said, "Much better than all those soppy roses and things that people usually decorate cakes with".

There was a family called Adams who lived where Daphne Wyatt now lives. He was an old man with a white beard and looked like Moses I thought. He was a typical Victorian, head-of-the-family type who expected the womenfolk to stop at home and wait on him. I suspect that my mother privately agreed with me that he was a pompous old boor. His wife was years younger than he was and helped look after his daughter by his first wife. In fact daughter and stepmother were good friends and when able to do so they played tennis together at Hoarwithy Club and were more like sisters. Eventually Nancie, the daughter, worked for father doing the accounts etc. I think the old man had died by then. Nancie had courage and she finally took the plunge and went to London and trained as a nurse and subsequently married and as the saying goes, "did well for herself".

The Pardington family were well known in Hoarwithy. I have mentioned them before and now that Rita (Edmonds) has sold the house that is the end of another era, though of course there are plenty of them still scattered around the district.

The row of cottages down on the road near Quarry Bank saw Barbara Langford's family, the Owens, grow up and move off and then there was a very old lady in the end cottage called Mrs Andrews who used to tell of the great flood of eighteen hundred and something when the river came right up to the bedroom windows of that row of cottages. I have since wondered if that was the occasion when the first dam built in the Claerwen Valley above Rhyader broke and released enormous quantities of water down the valley.

Quarry Bank was occupied by a retired Colonel, whose name I forget, but he had a small smooth-haired terrier dog. He had soldiered in far-flung lands where it was very hot, so the dog wore a specially made coat. He lost this coat one day and the colonel let it be known that a reward would be paid for its return. Thereafter rumour had it that the local lads would lie in wait and lure the dog around the corner and remove his coat and then turn up at Quarry Bank and claim a reward.

As you can see, life was never dull in Hoarwithy for an observer of human behaviour.

CHAPTER THIRTY-SIX

Pass-times and the Village Hall

Hoarwithy had many young people both schoolchildren and young adults in and around the village and there was always plenty going on.

FOOTBALL: The Hoarwithy team, known as the Lilywhites, played in a local league and there were often matches on the sports meadow on Saturdays. I believe they were quite successful and had an interested following to shout and cheer them on.

CRICKET: Which logically followed on in the summer months was equally popular and successful. I can recall the cricket team and their opponents coming up across the meadow in front of the shop and going up to the Church Reading Room for tea after the match (or was it in the interval?). The wives and mothers always prepared a feast and the shop benefited as all the goods came from us – bread and butter and slab cake – large fruit cake in a rectangular shape for cutting – fish paste etc. for sandwiches and of course gallons of tea. All of it came from the shop.

Old Mr Williams from Llanfrother Farm was a very keen supporter and he used to come in his little pony and trap and park on the sidelines and shout encouragement to the footballers. The story goes that he got so excited one day that the pony took fright and bolted and nearly tipped him in the river.

TENNIS: The Hoarwithy and District Tennis Club was my father's choice as he was fond of tennis as a young man and I belonged too as a schoolgirl. It was held in the meadow in front of The Mill, which, in those days, was all one with the grounds of the house which used to be the actual mill. There were two courts and a so-called pavilion (more like a converted chicken house really).

As a club we played matches against other clubs in the county. Father was our chief means of transport and the team squashed into his old Ford (Model T?) and trundled off to far flung corners of the county on Saturday afternoons.

In winter there were always lots of indoor entertainments. A Whist Drive was favourite. The younger and more active folk danced and the middle-aged and elderly played whist. This was the best way to raise funds to support the sports clubs. Jumble sales did well in that direction too.

The Reverend Evans (not the late Michael Evans) who was vicar and lived in Hentland Vicarage then, was a kindly man and his daughter managed a local troupe of girl-guides. I was too young to come into the Guides.

Later on, Hoarwithy had a village hall on a flat bit of land opposite The Salmons and on the left of the lane which leads up to Redbrook Farm. It was called BENGATHA, a word made up from the initials of the men who clubbed together to build it. It was a wooden chalet-type building and was a fine venue for dances and concerts etc. for some years, but then, as now, gangs from the Forest of Dean and other places caused too many "rough houses" and it fell out of favour and was demolished after the war.

CHAPTER THIRTY-SEVEN

A Human Story

In the immediate pre-war years, the labour shortage was becoming more pronounced and when my father needed a new van driver he was obliged to advertise.

A number of applicants replied and he chose a young man, whom I shall call Bill Smith, from outside the area. Bill seemed very keen to get the job and was able to start with no delay. He was directed to apply for lodgings in a house across the river and started work. He soon learned his way around the district and got the hang of the job and all went well for a couple of weeks. Then one morning, our village policeman came to see father and broke the news that Bill was an ex-convict currently out on parole. Naturally, father asked what his crime had been and was told that he had been caught taking money from the insurance company for which he had worked.

Father's view was that Bill had stolen money, been caught, had served his prison sentence and paid for his crime and so should be given the chance to start again. He did not propose to do anything about it.

However, Bill had seen the policeman and as soon as he had gone Bill stomped into the office and said, "Alright, give me my cards and I'll go. This always happens to me when I try to get a job". My father told him his views on the matter and sent him back to work with a stern warning that the accounts system would show up any cheating on his part. So it was up to him to go straight and that he would be treated the same as the rest of the staff. Bill settled down, was soon able to rent a cottage and his wife came over and joined him. They later produced a baby son and lived happily in Hoarwithy until he was called up and entered the Army. His wife and baby went back to his home town (to stay with her mother, I think).

Bill obviously felt that my father cared for him and he wrote to him quite frequently, long letters telling all about basic training, going overseas and later about fighting in North Africa with the Desert Army. My father did his best to reply to these letters and kept him up-to-date with Hoarwithy affairs. Then suddenly, the letters stopped coming and we feared the worst.

Years later when father was retired, he got the shock of his life one day to run into Bill in Hereford.

They both gaped at each other and said in chorus, "I thought you were dead!" It transpired that someone had told Bill that "The man from Hoarwithy shop has died". But it was father's ex-partner, who had retired some years previously due to illness, who had died. Having sorted out that error, Bill and my father had a good yarn together. We were all pleased to hear that Bill had used his post-war gratuity to buy a second-hand motor coach and had built up a thriving business from that small beginning, being now the owner of a coach company

He and his wife were happily settled in their own home town. It was pure chance that he had come to Hereford on business that day and that he and my father had met each other. We were very pleased to have a happy ending after all. I have sometimes thought about Bill and wondered what would have become of him if my father like all the rest had refused to employ him.

WARTIME

CHAPTER THIRTY-EIGHT

Wartime

I think I have about exhausted my pre-war memories of Hoarwithy, so it is time to move on to the wartime era. My teenage years coincided with the rise of Adolf Hitler and like everyone in Britain at the time I viewed askance the happenings in Germany. When Mr Chamberlain came back from Munich with his famous "piece of paper" and the promise of "peace in our time" I greeted the news with joy and relief as did everyone else. Our euphoria was short-lived as it soon became obvious that peace was not to be and when Germany invaded Poland, whose sovereignty Britain had guaranteed, there was no alternative but to declare war on Germany.

I wonder sometimes what my parents must have felt. They had gone through World War 1 only twenty years previously and here it was, starting up all over again. I know I felt the foundations of our world were crumbling and the future was black and full of foreboding. But as we had no choice we just had to find the strength to face it.

Mr Chamberlain's intervention did buy time and to its credit, the government of the day had been working hard to prepare for war.

The reactivation of Rotherwas munitions factory was the obvious thing in this part of the country. The rabbits, which had had it all their own way in the earthworks around the buildings were evicted, the refurbishment of the plant got under way and it was soon in production again. The pace gradually accelerated as the war hotted up and it was eventually working flat-out around the clock.

Today the big industrial estate at Rotherwas is completely transformed. It occupies a large area of land on the outskirts of Hereford and contains a great number of factories and businesses. So it is difficult to visualise the big sprawling factory site that it once was. I think I am correct in saying that its principal function was filling shell-cases and bombs with explosives.

Obviously there was always the danger of explosion, due either to enemy action or mistakes in the factory. Therefore every building was placed at a distance from the next one and they were all surrounded by high earth banks to isolate them and limit the damage which could occur if an accident happened. I understand each building had its own air-raid shelter too.

The old railway line from Ross to Hereford passed beside the factory, so one was able to watch what went on. Later when the daily bus service through Hoarwithy from Ross to Hereford was established, I went to school by bus. When the munitions factory started to draw in workers from all around Hereford, our bus used to detour down to the factory to pick up workmen going home. They would all pile in and fill the empty seats and then stand in the aisle; no rules in those days about not accepting standing passengers. They were all crammed in somehow, twelve or fifteen standing sometimes. The old bus would creak and groan its way up The Wonder hill at walking pace. The crowd would slowly thin out as passengers alighted along the way and by Hoarwithy all would be seated.

The effect of this factory was to raise the standard of living for many families as the pay was good and to underpaid rural workers it was a real boon. It also meant that for the first time since the 1914–18 War there was a shortage of labour in this area. I suppose wars have always had this effect, but I doubt if many of us realized then that our lifestyle was about to change and forever.

CHAPTER THIRTY-NINE

Air-Raid Wardens

These were recruited from men in civilian life who were over the age of call-up, or in a reserved occupation, or physically unfit for active service. In nearly all cases, they worked at their normal occupations by day and became air-raid wardens in their spare time. They had to attend lectures to be taught what to do and also, of course, received large wads of instructions to learn. They were then launched onto the general public, complete with whistle, tin hat, armband and badge.

They were not all as unpleasant as Mr Hodges in "Dad's Army". Most of them worked long, tiring hours conscientiously doing their jobs. My father was one and I went around with him in the early days of the war and helped as he demonstrated the construction of air-raid shelters, how to wear a gas mask, how to recognise mustard or phosgene gas, how to deal with incendiary bombs and how the stirrup-pump worked.

According to father, the first-aid lectures they received from the District Nurse were quite hilarious at times. She taught them how to treat bleeding, fractures and burns and how to deliver a baby in an emergency. She showed them how to cross hands to make an emergency chair to lift a casualty unable to walk. She stressed the need to carry a length of cord at all times to use for tying an umbilical cord, or making a tourniquet. She would test them from time to time. For example:

Q: *"How would you cope with a badly wounded man?"*
A: *"Er...um...ah...I'd cross my hands with my mate like this (demonstrating) and we'd pick him up and run like hell"*
Q: *"What equipment would you always carry?"*
A: *"A piece of string"*

On the subject of bleeding, she was most emphatic that they had to know how to try and stop it. Therefore she showed them where the pressure points were and explained how to bandage properly and so on. On one occasion she hauled out a big tough-looking man and used him as a model to stand in front of the class. She asked them to imagine this man was wounded. How would they tackle the situation? The class was very slow in coming up with the answers, so she encouraged them saying, "Come on, here he is bleeding away, look at him! The blood is pouring down his arm, he's in great pain, he's going white and cold and faint. What are you going to do?"

Happening to glance at her model she saw he was on the verge of fainting as the full horror of her words took root. She worked hard did that nurse!

One of the principal duties of air-raid wardens was checking that all windows were properly blacked-out. The phrase "Put that light out" was one of the catch phrases of the war years and like traffic wardens today, they were not always popular when going on their rounds.

In the cities the A.R.P. did much really good work. They helped rescue people from the rubble of bombed buildings and directed the public to the shelters; they rendered first aid and generally helped direct traffic and so on.

There were not many "incidents" in Hoarwithy of course, but there were some and the wardens had to deal with them.

CHAPTER FORTY

Shortages and the Blackout

If you have watched "Dad's Army" on T.V., please believe me that the activities of Private Walker were very true to life.

Every aspect of daily life was affected by shortages. Cigarettes were sometimes scarce and difficult to track down, but it was the ordinary commodities, which were utterly taken for granted before the war, which seemed to vanish. Things like safety pins, collar studs, Kirby grips, elastic, shampoo and countless other things. If one complained, the inevitable reply was: "Don't you know there's a war on!" Which got one down.

The natural result of this state of affairs was that the shop keepers tended not to display goods which were in short supply. They went "under the counter" to be carefully doled out to regular customers. Hence the old joke, "How often do I have to be refused before I become a regular customer?"

Newspapers were rationed to quantity of newsprint, so therefore most of them dwindled to about four to six double pages only, which meant there was not as much news to read and what was printed tended to be facts briefly stated with no long rambling articles like today's papers.

The BBC would say things like, "There was an air-raid in the Midlands today. We lost two planes and the Luftwaffe had four shot down".Anything broadcast had to be monitored in case important details were released which could help the enemy to evaluate what damage they had inflicted and where. The announcers would give their names so that people knew them and that they were genuine BBC announcers. There was no other channel to broadcast on then on radio and of course there was no T.V..

The "Blackout" was an important part of wartime life. All windows had to be covered with blackout curtains or shutters before any lights were turned on. Shops, pubs and cinemas usually had some sort of screen door between the outside door and the interior so that people could come and go without showing any lights.

Out of doors it was permissible to carry a torch or lantern provided it was not directed upwards or waved about in any way that might be seen from the air. All traffic lights had shades over them and the light restricted to a slit by covering the glass with black material. All cars and lorries had their headlights dimmed to a slit.

Street lights were painted blue and were either absent or very dim. So in towns at night it was either great fun, or an awful nuisance, to grope around in the darkened streets according to which age group you belonged to.

In the countryside it had always been dark, so it did not make much difference. Father was able to get some supplies of black material for making blackout curtains and most people blacked out their living-rooms and kitchens. But it was expensive and difficult to do all the widows in a house and many people relied on their ordinary curtains and a very dim night-light for other rooms, or just groped around in the dark.

In our case, my parents had three big windows in their bedroom so mostly just drew their ordinary curtains and made do with a very dim night-light.

My mother being a light sleeper, was usually awakened by their alarm and would dig my father in the ribs to put the electric kettle on. When it boiled she would poke him again, he would make the tea and hand her a cup. Having drunk their tea, they would creep out of bed to face another day's start in the dark.

She complained one morning that the tea was very weak, but was assured by my father that he had put in the usual spoonful of tea and that she was imagining it. However, when mother went upstairs later in the day to make the bed, she found that the teapot was innocent of even one tea-leaf, but that there was a spoonful of tea-leaves on the floor beside it! Poor father, I guess he had to listen to her then.

CHAPTER FORTY-FIVE

Air Raids

I am sure you have all seen plenty of T.V. programmes about the air-raids in the big cities, but I think Hoarwithy's experiences are worth recording as well.

The sirens which warned of the approach of enemy aircraft were sited in towns in prominent positions on top of buildings and were audible for quite a distance. The warning sound was a repetitive rising and falling note, a sort of fiendish wailing noise, whilst the All Clear was a continuous note, similar to a normal factory hooter today (though on second thoughts, do factories have hooters today?).

Do not forget that before the advent of "the wireless" with its time-signals, people had no certainty of the correct time. Many relied on someone coming from town who had checked his watch against the Town Hall clock; hence factory hooters!

Hoarwithy was too far away from Ross or Hereford to hear the sirens unless the wind carried the sound faintly to us. There was obviously nothing here to attract the attention of enemy bombers, but having said that, we were under the flight path of bombers going to, or perhaps more importantly, coming from raids on the big cities such as Birmingham, Bristol or Cardiff. These planes sometimes had to jettison their bombs and so we did have some bombs fall in this area.

I can remember going across a ploughed field opposite Hoarwithy in the grounds of Aramstone to look at a bomb crater and doubtless there were others.

One lucky (or from our viewpoint, unlucky) hit, was a bomb that landed on Kilforge House up above Carey. It damaged the staircase amongst other things and the occupant was marooned upstairs. She was an elderly lady and was rescued by her gardener-chauffeur who put up a ladder to the bedroom window and helped her to get out. The story goes that he tried to persuade her to seek shelter elsewhere for the night, but she came down the ladder clutching her jewel-case and firmly announced that she was not going to let some upstart German painter drive her out of her house and refused to go anywhere.

Hereford's Munitions Factory was a legitimate target and several attempts were made to destroy it, but with very little success, or so we thought at the time, but I have recently learnt that there were some direct hits on the Rotherwas Munitions Factory, with some loss of life. We were told that it was not easy to identify from the air as it was often obscured by river mist. In those pre-smokeless days, Hereford, being in a hollow, suffered greatly from really dense fogs at times. I remember many times going to school when the river mists would lift to give a bright sunny day in Hoarwithy, but our school in Hereford was dark and foggy all day.

In early autumn, the Nazis took to dropping incendiary bombs on the cornfields or just scattering them about anywhere in the hope of starting fires. The Home Guard of course, had already checked that every household had buckets of sand and a shovel, all ready to deal promptly with those things. The idea was to cover the bombs with sand to put out the fire. Any fire that did start would be dealt with initially by local stirrup-pumps.

In the cities the Fire Brigades were augmented by the A.F.S. (Auxiliary Fire Service) and between them they fought valiantly to put out fires. Hoarwithy used its stirrup-pumps to good advantage as a first line of defence until Ross Fire Fighters could get here.

I shall relate in another chapter the saga of the fire-bomb that landed on our roof. I went away soon after the start of the war and was in London for many of the air-raids, more of that in the next chapter.

CHAPTER FORTY-SIX

London Air-Raids

I went away from Hoarwithy soon after the start of the war and was staying with a cousin in London when the first air-raid occurred.

We lay awake cowering in our beds waiting for something dreadful to happen; absolutely nothing happened. We heard later that it was a false alarm. However, later in the war we had air-raids every night during the winter months, two or three alarms in one night sometimes.

First, of course, came the sirens, then the bang-bang of the anti-aircraft guns. If you looked out you could see searchlights probing the sky. Then followed the sounds of aircraft and the whistle and crack of bombs. The noise could be far away, or come closer and fade and then return; it would all come and go and then eventually the All-Clear and silence.

I was living in the Nurses' Home at this time and we had the option of staying put or going down to the basement passages and sleeping on metal bunk-beds. Most nurses preferred to stay where they were in a warm bed. We worked hard for long hours and were tired at night, needing our sleep. The alternative of going down to the discomfort of the dark and cold, with the possibility of being buried by a direct hit, did not appeal.

This situation gradually brings home to you the realization that there is no certainty in life and that there was absolutely nothing to be done about it. It was therefore a futile waste of time to worry about it. I know I usually slept peacefully through all the alarms and excursions of the night.

I did quite a lot of night-duty during these years and I did find it upsetting on the Children's Ward trying to reassure the little ones when an air-raid started. They would all be awakened by the sirens and would start crying and calling out to me. It was hard to comfort them as I could not cuddle them all at once.

I felt sorry for the adult patients too, as many of them were bed-bound. One feels much more helpless tied to a bed and unable to run.

All this had its lighter side of course. One night I was creeping quietly across the Women's Ward carrying a pile of metal bed-pans to place handy for the morning, when I fell over an examination couch which I had not seen in the gloom, because it was covered by a dark coloured cover. I dropped the bed-pans with a deafening clatter, which of course woke all the ladies. I apologised to them most abjectly and they settled down again, eventually.

In the morning one of the men in the Men's Ward opposite asked me whereabouts in the hospital had last night's bomb landed and had it done much damage. When I assured him that there had been no bomb, but that the crash he had heard was caused by my dropping a pile of bed-pans, he refused to believe me. He thought I was trying to spare him the truth.

"Even Nurse Russill (me) couldn't make that much noise", he said. I will conclude this London episode by mentioning the hospital's Chaplain. He was an elderly Scotsman, attached, I think, to the local parish church. He came every night to every ward in the hospital. He walked quietly around and spoke a few words to each patient in turn and then would ask us to pause for a few moments while he stood in the centre of the ward and called for God's blessing on us all and prayed that we might be kept safe from the dangers of the night. We all said the Lord's Prayer and he would bless us all and go off smartly to the next ward. I felt that the patients must have found great comfort in his words and in his presence.

CHAPTER FORTY-SEVEN

Food Rationing

The pre-war government had been busy making plans for food rationing well before the war started. In this respect they did learn a lesson from the First World War, when food riots were experienced. They were determined to start rationing when the war broke out and they did. It took only a week or two.

My father had been quietly buying extra goods for a long time, so he had enough stock to supply everyone during the first few weeks, whilst the wholesalers were more or less closed down while they got their act together.

Hoarwithy shop suddenly found itself the centre of attraction to shoppers from Ross and other places, all trying to buy up sugar and so on. My father quickly put a stop to that by refusing to sell more than 2 lbs to strangers, as he wished to conserve his stocks for his own customers.

Every person in the land was issued with an identity card and a ration book and was required to register with the grocer, baker and milkman, in order to buy weekly rations. The shopkeepers in turn registered their customers with their local food office. I am not sure, but I think the Ross Food Office was in the Market Hall. (Does anyone remember?).

The Local Food Offices were presumably run by the county who were ultimately responsible to the Ministry of Food. Each shopkeeper had to clip out the coupons and points from the customer's ration book and send them to the Local Food Office, which I suppose, authorised them to buy further supplies from their wholesalers. The Ministry of Food decided which foods were to be rationed and how much each person could have.

The basic essentials such as butter, sugar, tea and flour had coupons specified in the ration book; other items such as tinned pilchards, corned beef, dried fruit, baked beans, tinned fruit and jam were "on points".

Each ration book had so many points and the goods were assessed at so many points each tin, or packet and customers could spend their points as they wished and according to what items were available.

At the start of rationing, the quantities were not too bad and most families managed quite well. But the quantity slowly became less and there were times when life was irksome as the daily diet became very monotonous. So much shipping was being lost that not all that much food was reaching us. I heard that at one point it was reckoned there was no more than six weeks supply in the country, even on strict rations.

Can you today visualise a tea ration of about 2 oz per person per week; small quantities of butter and margarine and bread and potatoes and about a quarter of a pound of stewing beef and enough cheese to fit in a mousetrap? There were no bananas (they disappeared early on) and probably no oranges or apples. You got

83

cabbage if you were lucky, but food was monotonous. We did not starve, but it was not exciting eating.

Many people used their sugar ration to make jam which helped to brighten the bread and margarine. War-time margarine was pretty horrible stuff, not like today's.

Bakers were quickly put on to "National Flour" and told to bake only standard-sized loaves, so all the interesting recipes and shapes that were on offer pre-war all vanished and standard loaves of a sort of greyish wholemeal were all the bakers could produce. Rumours were rife about some of the ingredients of this flour. Supposedly, they included other types of grain as well as wheat and things like French chalk.

Bread was rationed sometimes, but not all the time and not too severely. Potatoes were rationed sometimes, but again mostly there were enough.

Then there was the dreaded "powdered egg". Some weeks there were not enough shell-eggs for us all to have our ration, so we had "dried egg" egg powder. Obviously it was easier to import packets of powder, than shell-eggs, so one followed the instructions for reconstituting the powder and tried to enjoy one's "scrambled egg" and imagine it was a real egg.

Rationing meant a lot of extra work for the shopkeepers and for the customers and it did not end in 1945. It dragged on for years after the war because the country was bankrupt and shipping was very scarce after all the war-time sinkings and as a nation we could not buy much food from abroad. I think it finally finished in 1955, as I can definitely remember briefly having a ration book for my son as a baby.

CHAPTER FORTY-EIGHT

One Incendiary Bomb

Stirrup-pumps were the first line of defence, as I have mentioned. I think the general public was urged to buy them and many did. I suppose they were cheaper to make than sophisticated fire-extinguishers. They looked a bit like an old-fashioned tyre-pump, with a tube for spraying water at one side and another tube with an inlet valve which rested in a bucket or tin bath of water at the other. One person pumped and the other person sprayed the fire. They were quite effective in a small way. People were encouraged to keep the pump and water receptacle in a convenient place.

My parents placed theirs in the attic, reasoning that the roof was probably the most vulnerable place. In any case, there were plenty of buckets downstairs and two large rain-water tanks. Now we had an indoor cat at this time and she was expecting kittens and was roaming around looking for a suitable place to have them, my mother made a bed for her in an old box and put her up in the attic for the night, as being a quiet and secluded place where nothing could upset her.

In the middle of the night, mother awoke to the noise of an aircraft and became aware of bright lights. She woke father and they looked out to see where the bombs had landed. They smelled smoke and suddenly realized their own roof was on fire. The bomb had rolled down into a gully in the back part of the roof and was burning furiously. They rushed up the attic stairs to find that the bomb was melting the lead flashing on the floor of the gully and the molten lead was dripping through the roof onto the rafters which were smouldering.

My father grabbed the stirrup-pump and exhorting mother to pump, he set-to to spray the fire (they had rehearsed this and worked well as a team). The attic filled with smoke and steam as they battled away. It seemed an age before the flames began to die down. Mother said she was exhausted, but the fear of loosing her home kept her going. She said she remembered at some stage seeing our pregnant cat dash past her like a streak of lightening and disappearing down the stairs. Fleetingly Mother thought the experience should precipitate matters for her.

At last their efforts paid off and the fire went out. Only then did they become aware of voices and banging and realized that people were at the door shouting out to them. They went down and let them in. It was a small crowd of neighbours who had seen the fire and had come to help. They had also sent for the fire-brigade, which arrived shortly afterwards. The firemen went on the roof and checked that all was properly out and no fear of a flare-up. Mother finished up by making cocoa for everyone and slowly became aware that the neighbours, like themselves, were mostly in their night-clothes and overcoats and lacking false teeth etc. It all seemed a bit unreal to her.

When the firemen were satisfied, they went back to Ross and the neighbours drifted home leaving my parents to get dressed and start a new day, thankful that the damage was no worse than a hole in the roof. (No, the cat did not give birth until several days later.).

CHAPTER FORTY-NINE

Evacuees

Hoarwithy received its share of evacuees: an infant school from a working class district of Birmingham. I can recall them arriving in the village, by bus I think. Their teachers were evacuated with them and took care of them. The village "elders" organised cars to take them around to their adopted homes. I recall a lot of noise and confusion. These city children were so shrill and noisy compared with the local, rural children. However, it must have been very well organised really, because in no time at all, the children were all installed in their new homes.

Most of the village families took them in with open hearts and tried their best to make them feel loved and wanted. However, it was a bit of a culture shock for some.

The government had laid down certain guidelines. Parents were supposed to send their children off properly dressed and with the rest of their clothes, toys and so on packed up with them and of course their gas-masks and ration books. The real parents were supposed to contribute to the child's upkeep by their foster-parents. (There were no state allowances for children then.). Many parents more than fulfilled their obligations, but some did not and a few deliberately tried to dump their children permanently.

Some of the village parents were shocked to find that the evacuees had no clothes or belongings with them and that they were very poorly and inadequately dressed, with no underwear etc. and what clothes they had were worn and filthy.

It soon became apparent that many of the children had never sat down at a table and eaten a proper cooked dinner. They were accustomed to running around with a slice of bread and jam or a packet of chips. Many were prone to bed-wetting.

Some of the parents in Birmingham made great efforts to travel down to see their children, or write to them; but some did not bother very much.

It caused some resentment when a foster-mother who scrimped and saved to try to feed and clothe these city children was confronted by the real parents who rolled up in their own car, mother in a fur coat and father prosperous looking, explaining that they were now both free to work (probably in munitions) and were therefore earning very good money and able to afford luxuries that Hoarwithy workers could only dream of.

To start with, the teachers were allocated the Reading Room as a school and they tried their best to cope, but it was not satisfactory. I think that later, when many children had returned to Birmingham, the evacuees were able to go to Hentland School with the Hoarwithy children.

Mr and Mrs Evan Jones who lived at "The New Harp" then, had always hankered after a family. They were delighted to be given a little girl to care for. I think she was called Betty. They adored her on sight and took great pleasure in dressing her in pretty clothes and indulging her and showing her to everyone with such joy. Inevitably, when her real parents came and claimed her back eventually, they were heart-broken.

Mrs Hitchcocks, who lived next door to my present home, had several children. She struggled to feed and clothe them and loved them dearly. Coincidently, one day recently a middle-aged man appeared next door and since there was no-one in at the time, he called across the hedge to me and asked if I had known Mrs Hitchcocks. When I said, "Yes", he came up and told me how he had been evacuated there during the war and how he had promised himself to come back one day. We had quite a talk and off he went.

My contact with the evacuee children at the time was with the ones who came to the shop. They did not think much of it because we did not sell ice-cream (no freezer cabinet then) or chips and only ordinary chewing-gum. They, in their Birmingham accents, were demanding "Boublegoum", at least that is what it sounded like and we had never heard of it. The refinements of bubblegum had not then reached darkest Herefordshire.

My father had been presented with a wrist-watch pre-war for promoting Wrigley's Chewing—Gum and I remember him saying that if only the evacuees had arrived a year or two sooner, Wrigleys might have thought him worth a grandfather-clock!

It must have been a shock to these little inner-city infants to be suddenly transported to rural Herefordshire; to find that milk came from great big cows and not in nice clean bottles from the dairy and that at night the roads were pitch-dark with no streetlights and that at the Red Rail end of the village there was no electricity at all. There was no cinema and only one shop and to cap it all, that did not sell "Bouble Goum"

CHAPTER FIFTY

Evacuees 2

There was another school evacuated to our area, though this was not government-sponsored; it was a private arrangement.

Our vicar here in Hentland Parish was the Reverend Mr Massey. He came here in about 1936 I think, from some inner-city parish where he had worked very hard and suffered from ill health. He was directed here, so that he could rest and regain his health in quiet rural surroundings.

He was married, with several small children and I expect he found it a bit of a struggle financially living in Hentland Vicarage. In those days it was a great barn of a place with outbuildings, stables, orchards and so on and must have cost a fortune in upkeep. There were no children's allowances then, of course. Today the house is actually Kynaston Court, our local residential home and the stables and outbuildings have been hived off to make quite large, attractive houses.

Mr Massey was a very lively and energetic vicar and always willing to visit people and join in village events. I remember he kept a pig and was always grateful to local farmers when they gave him a load of swedes or anything for the pig.

When war broke out he made an arrangement with a private boarding school from Kent. I do not know how they came in contact, but a happy arrangement was agreed that the school, the teachers, pupils, domestics, etc. moved into the vicarage, leaving the Massey family a small part of the house. In return the school accepted the Massey children as pupils.

My father was amused on one occasion when he visited Mr Massey. They both came out and stood on the doorstep just as the children all came out for playtime. Mr Massey remarked, "Ah, it's a wise father that knows his own children", as they both surveyed the crowd of youngsters rushing about.

One of the big houses in Kings Caple was commandeered as a boarding home for those Birmingham evacuees who were not suitable for placement in private homes. Yes, the government had the power to commandeer premises during wartime if they needed them!

These children were misfits. Some had already been placed in private homes and then retuned as being unmanageable. Some were persistent bedwetters, or suffered from skin complaints, fits or other problems. They had a trained staff to care for them, but some of the Big House staff from pre-war days, such as gardeners, remained. The old gardener, who lived in a cottage nearby, was most upset by the way these children ran wild all over the grounds. When he caught one of them stealing peaches from one of the greenhouses, he dealt with him in the traditional way, by giving him a good walloping.

He was somewhat taken aback when the Matron scolded him and forbade him to touch any of the children. She apparently gave him a talk on child psychology and on how damaged these children were. He later confided in my father and explained that, "It was this here psychology is what's wrong with them little so-and-so's" Father said he thought the gardener had decided that psychology was some illness akin to measles!

Many city families with friends or relatives in the country made their own private arrangements, of course, but schools en bloc moved from the cities to the countryside away from the bombing.

Hereford High School for Girls, which I had attended, doubled up with an evacuated school. I believe one school attended in the morning and the other in the afternoon, thus sharing the building and facilities between them and each doing more studying at home to make up for lost time. I do not know how all this worked out but it was a reasonable alternative to staying in the cities.

CHAPTER FIFTY-ONE

Manpower Shortages

As the war progressed, more and more people were called up and the age group
for call-up got older and older. Consequently, in "civvy street" many businesses
were manned by pensioners, married women or unfit categories such as poor
eyesight, heart disease, flat feet and what-have-you.

Towards the end of the war, those aged forty were called up including married
women. They were only exempt if they had young children to care for. This caused
a bit of a "baby-boom" amongst older married women. The children were known as
"Bevin babies" after Ernest Bevan the Employment Minister.

Women of course, replaced men in the factories, in transport, in schools and on
the land and in many jobs that had been all male before the war. My cousin, who was
a language teacher, worked in a Boys Grammar School in Birmingham. The
understanding was that the women would step down when the men returned. I know
it gave me quite a shock to find that the Railway Porters on Paddington Station were
all women. (Yes, there were Railway Porters pre-war who actually carried your
luggage for you; no trolleys in those days for you to use yourself.).

In Hoarwithy, my father had of course lost his younger workers and had to rely on
the older ones and married women. Mrs Hardy, who until recently, used to live at
Red Rail, drove a bread van at one stage I remember, as well as being "Farmer's
Wife" at Llanfrother Farm. Old Walter Newport had left the bakehouse and his
assistant was called up, so father had to do the baking himself with what help he could
get. It was a long day for him. He started at 6 am and finished in the bakehouse about
11am and then had to start in the shop. Then at 6pm back he went to the bakehouse
to mix the dough for the following morning. He also had duties as Air-Raid Warden.

The local Labour Exchange did their best for him but youngsters were soon called
up and the older generation were all working hard. He thought he had struck lucky
when Dianna arrived. She was an out-of-work ballet dancer. She and her mother had
fled the bombing and taken lodgings at Altbough Farm. However, she soon proved
hopeless. She was often late and was not much good at the job. She complained she
had sprained her wrist lifting bread tins and expected father to do it all himself. He
finally insisted that she either pulled her weight or got a sick note from the doctor,
so that he could try and replace her.

She went off to see Dr Green. He was on the point of retirement when war broke
out. He was not too well and limped badly from a World War 1 injury. He had had
two sons, one of them had been killed in fighting (in North Africa, I think), the other
was missing, believed killed. As you can guess, he was not very sympathetic towards
Dianna. In fact it was reported on the village grapevine that he shouted to her to get
out. He told her there was nothing wrong with her and that she should be ashamed

of herself. Good men were fighting and dying to protect the likes of her and she could not even be bothered to do her little bit to help her country and he never wanted to see her again.

It was at this point that my mother stepped into the breach and became baker's assistant. So they both rose at 5.30 am to start at 6pm in the bakehouse. (since Summer Time remained all the year round and in the actual summer there was Double Summer Time, it was then really 3.30 when they got up.).

I came home on leave to find the house covered in a fine film of flour dust and hardly saw my parents at all. Looking back on those days it seems queer to remember how "unemployment" was a word erased from the dictionary, as it were!

CHAPTER FIFTY-TWO

Wartime Shopkeeping

Wartime saw a big change in the running of food shops. Each customer had to register with a grocer, butcher, greengrocer and so on and to purchase their rations they had to surrender the necessary coupons. Money was not so much the problem as finding the goods to buy.

In towns, customers tended to take their ration books with them and queue for whatever was going. Many country customers, who probably did not actually get to the shops, tended to leave their coupons with the shopkeeper. Most shopkeepers tried to distribute what they had as fairly as they could and divide any extras without being asked. The customers accepted gratefully anything that was offered.

If customers became disenchanted with any tradesman, they could change to another one, but it had to be done via their Local Food Office. This effectively spiked the guns of those people who, pre-war, had run up a fair sized bill with one shopkeeper and then left him on some trumped-up charge and proceeded to repeat the process with some rival shop.

The administrators in the Food Office had soon rumbled this trick and would ask the customer: "Why do you want to change? Do you owe any money?" and "What is your complaint against your present shopkeeper?" and so on. If the answer was, "Yes", they did owe money (the Food Office would check with the shopkeepers), they would be told, "When you have paid your debts you can change". The customers might find then that the other shops did not want their custom and it might not be so easy to change as they had thought.

The wholesalers could not divide such things as butter, sugar and tea exactly and tended to make up the rations to the nearest block of butter or tea-chest-sized box of tea, or dozen packs of sugar packets. Therefore a surplus would build up and my father would wait until he had enough to give every household an extra bag of sugar, or ration of butter. He had to keep enough in hand to supply services personnel or other workers who lived away and came home on leave. Servicemen had a week or weekend Ration Card to bring home, whatever was appropriate.

Inspectors from the Food Office visited the shops from time to time to check up on the way they were being run. Obviously, human nature being what it is, there were black market traders around. I expect a van-load of rations sold in the East End of London, or any other big city, would make a very good profit.

There was a sticky situation one day when a lady charged into Hoarwithy Shop and loudly demanded to know why her sister in Kings Caple had had an extra packet of sugar and she had not. Was her village to get it next week? Everyone tried to hush her up, because a quiet little man in the corner was suspected of being from the Food Office. We never heard any more, so either he had not heard what she said, or he was not prepared to ask about it. Or perhaps he was not from the Food Office after all. Who knows?

CHAPTER FIFTY-THREE

Food

Under rationing there was not a lot of choice and housewives had to work hard trying to feed their families on what was available to them.

Lord Woolton (the owner of Lewis's Store in Liverpool) was appointed to head the Ministry of Food, a wartime set-up and he really did organise the nation's food rationing very well.

He published numerous recipes and hints for the housewife; Woolton Pie comes to mind. It was a pie made from mixed vegetables and flavoured with an Oxo Cube (no meat, you see, but filling!).

Another winner was a pie dish of mashed potato with a dab of margarine, sprinkled with grated cheese. There were numerous recipes using dried egg powder. Such things as tinned pilchards and baked beans were a sought-after delicacy. Fruit and vegetables were available in season, but bananas of course, vanished and oranges were sometimes non-existent. Sweets and chocolates dwindled to perhaps one small bar of chocolate now and then. Many families nobly saved this for their children.

Horse-meat was sometimes for sale, but was not viewed with favour by most people. Whale meat came to the butchers' shops at one stage and was tolerated by the public. There were of course, the inevitable jokes like, "Mother says: can we have the head for the cat?"

Fish was unobtainable, when the shops did have any to sell and I suspect that some of the cod's heads were used for making fish-cakes instead of feeding the cat. The fish and chip shops flourished and were open when they had the fish and potatoes to work on. Many people were pleased to be able to buy a meal of fish and chips if they were going out in the evening.

British restaurants were a wartime invention and were very popular with the public. Ordinary restaurants were not allowed to give more than one meat course per person and were heavily reliant on game and rabbit.

They were generally pretty expensive anyway and much hedged about with rules and regulations. The British Restaurants were a type of non-profit-making, largely voluntary set-up. They were sited in town centres and bombed areas where workpeople had little choice in feeding themselves. On entering one paid for tokens and then spent them as one wished. I think you were entitled to one main course and either soup or sweet or a cup of tea. I cannot really remember the various options but I do know one could get quite a satisfying meal.

I was reminded of the British Restaurants when I was in Perugia in Italy and procured my main meal of the day in the "Mensa Comunale", which was a sort of Local Council Canteen open to anyone wanting a reasonable feed away from the tourist trail.

I worked in hospitals for most of the war years and nurses in those days were fed and housed by the hospital. We were given some of our sugar ration, our butter ration and some of our margarine and tea rations and were forced to use them as we wished. We put out our pots and jars each week to have these rations doled out to us. At meal times, each nurse buttered her bread or sugared her tea to suit herself.

When we were evacuated out to the countryside (near Basingstoke) where our patients were sent to get them out of London, we were able to go blackberrying and made jam with farm apples and blackberries and our sugar rations. Thus we were able to spread jam on our bread and margarine. This is not relevant to Hoarwithy, but I expect many of the younger people from the village had similar experiences wherever they were at the time.

I do not remember whether Hereford had a British Restaurant. I expect they did; the workers had to be fed!

CHAPTER FIFTY-FOUR

Farming

Farmers during the war (and for some years afterwards) were Very Important People! The nation had to be fed and since shipping was needed for war purposes and an alarming number of ships were being sunk by German U-Boats, it was glaringly obvious that the pre-war imports of cheap food had to cease and the British had to provide as much as possible of their own food.

Farmers were exhorted to grow more and the public encouraged to try and grow as much as they could, either on allotments or in their own gardens and backyards. "Dig for Victory" was the slogan of the day. Most people in Hoarwithy already grew their own vegetables etc., but people in the towns and cities took to the idea with a will. Town Councils ploughed up public parks for potatoes and grazed animals on open spaces. I can remember seeing sheep grazing in Hyde Park. (I wonder whether some of them disappeared into the Black Market?). We were told that the famous playing fields of Eton were dug for potatoes.

Ordinary citizens grew things in tubs and kept an odd hen or two in the back-yard in the industrial towns and everyone tried to do a little bit.

I heard somewhere that at the outbreak of war it was estimated that about a half of our foodstuffs were home-grown and the other half imported. By the end of the war, we were as a nation, almost self-supporting. I do not know how true that was, but certainly everyone tried. One saw little patches of vegetables on gun-sites and wherever there was a plot of earth or someone to cultivate it. An organisation was set up to help co-ordinate the farmers' efforts. Each County had its own Agricultural Committee, with powers to direct farmers. In extreme cases, where a farm was being badly managed, they would step in and give the management of that farm to someone else. I suspect it was also part of their job, in partnership with the Ministry of Labour, to ensure that the farmers had the help they needed to do the job properly. Some farm workers had joined the Forces, but most were classified as being in a "reserved occupation" and had to stay in farming. Even so, there was a shortage of farm workers, particularly for harvesting and so the Land Army came into being.

The Land Army was made up of women who underwent training for working on the land and many were city girls who presumably preferred this to joining the Forces. They worked hard and certainly did their bit, learning how to drive tractors, milk cows and so on. The wives and daughters of many farmers also did this kind of work, of course. Jean Hodges told me the other day that she drove a tractor for her father on Lower Penalt Farm in Kings Caple.

Students from Universities and Colleges also had to work during their vacations usually in harvesting of some sort. A cousin of mine who was at Aberystwyth University was sent to harvest potatoes in Herefordshire. She used to come here to my parents' home for a hot bath and a rest on Sundays. In those days the sophisticated machines which turn over the earth and load potatoes all in one movement had not been invented. She said that a tractor and digger went around uprooting the potato plants and the girls were each given a sector of field to rush in and bag all the potatoes thus revealed and be ready to do this each time the tractor came their way. It was back breaking work and allowed very little time before the machine came round again. Her friend was sent to Much Marcle and stayed in a hostel there. She, I believe was either hop-picking or fruit-picking.

Another source of labour, of course, was prisoners of war; they came later in the war; more of them in the next chapter.

CHAPTER FIFTY-FIVE

P.O.W.'s and Foreign Troops

When war started all enemy nationals were sorted out. Spies were imprisoned (some were executed I believe) and the rest were interned, mostly in the Isle of Man. As fighting started, prisoners were taken and they were put into Prisoner of War Camps.

I presume some sort of grading took place and many were put to work on the land (and maybe other jobs as well; I do not know about that). But I do know that a German prisoner was sent to the farm of my school-friend's family at Preston-on-Wye. He helped with the farm work and was treated like any other farm worker by the family. They found out that he was a painter and decorator by trade, so strictly hush-hush and against the rules, he and the farmer arranged that he decorated the house when things were quiet on the farm.

I used to cycle across country to visit my friend's family at times and that was how I came to know that there was an Italian P.O.W. Camp at Wormelow and the inmates worked on the farms in that area. I saw groups of men waiting to be picked up by the Camp Bus to return for their evening meal. They wore a very distinctive brown uniform, so were easy to recognise. Initially, I was very surprised to see them at large in the countryside, quite unguarded. I thought, "What is to stop them from escaping?" then, of course I realised that Britain being an Island, there was nowhere for them to escape to and in any case they were probably quite contented to work on a farm in rural England and wait for the war to end. They were well out of the fighting and were being fed and cared for, so why should they want to go back?

I heard recently of one farming family who kept up an acquaintanceship with the Italian family of their Prisoner of War and the two families visit each other today.

There were many foreign troops in Britain during the war years: Free French, Czechoslovaks, Dutch, Norwegians and so on. A few came as far as Hoarwithy, but it was the Americans who overwhelmed this country later on. They did penetrate everywhere. We had jeeploads of them even here. They visited local families and tried to pick up local girls.

Americans were very well paid in comparison with our troops; their uniforms were made of superior fabrics and they were generally better dressed and fed. They came with gifts such as chocolate, nylon stockings, tins of spam etc., so it was understandable that they generated some jealousy among the British troops, most of whom were fighting in Africa, on the high sea or in a number of unpleasant theatres of war. "Overpaid, oversexed and over here", was the slogan which described the Yanks. Of course, they in their turn went and fought in Europe and elsewhere and without them we would not have won the war. In the first critical days of the Allied landings in Europe the American Forces suffered very heavy casualties.

Many British girls did form serious friendships with Americans and married them and after the war G.I. Brides sailed on the Queen Mary and other passenger liners for new homes in America.

CHAPTER FIFTY-SIX

Transport in War-Time Hoarwithy: Part One

Oil is vital to our economy and in war-time doubly so, especially since we had no oil industry of our own, then. Fortunately, we did have a flourishing coal industry which fuelled our war effort; but as oil had to be imported it was very strictly rationed right from the beginning.

Car owners had a minute amount which gave them only enough for one or two short trips a year. Farmers and businesses and commercial vehicle operators had an allowance which was deemed necessary for their needs. Some petrol was coloured with a dye which was easily detectable to deter sales of it on the black market.

There were plenty of trains and buses compared with today's public transport, so it was possible to get about if necessary. However, the slogan, "Is your journey really necessary? Was the order of the day to discourage would-be travellers.

Trains were mostly steam-trains and they usually managed to run to schedule. But the enemy had a habit of bombing the lines and trains if they could manage it and so our trains were sometimes diverted, stopped or damaged.

As you can imagine, a train at night shows up from the air like a fiery caterpillar, so all lighting in carriages had to be blacked out. The blinds on the windows had to be drawn down and the light-bulbs were painted dark blue, so that there was only enough illumination to grope one's way to a seat. Sometimes, if an air-raid was in progress, the lights would be switched off altogether.

I recall going back to London after a break at home in Hoarwithy, when we were all made to change to another train at Reading. I do not know why, but I, with all the rest, was packed into this other train in total darkness and I travelled to Paddington sitting on someone's lap. I got the impression that the carriage was full of soldiers by their conversation, but we none of us saw each other because everywhere was pitch dark.

Coming home from Paddington, the trains were always jam-packed to start with and I often spent half the journey sitting on my suitcase in the corridor.

One incident concerning trains, which made a vivid impression on me was seeing a train taking munitions workers from the night-shift at Rotherwas Munitions Factory to, I presume, Ross or maybe further. I was waiting on the platform at Ballingham to catch a train to London. It was morning, the sun was shining brightly, when suddenly the train popped out of the tunnel and rushed past. The sunshine illuminated every detail of the interior and I could see it was packed full with workers, all of whom were a hideous yellow-brown colour from working with explosives in the factory. They were all fast asleep, sprawled in their seats like zombies. It was like a scene from a horror movie, showing a train-load of hideous corpses. I presume they would have gone home, washed, rested and tackled their normal chores and then returned to Rotherwas for another night of filling shells or bombs. War-time meant a long, hard, never-ending grind for many workers.

Farmers had long, hard days of work too and they tried to find ways of getting into town now and then for a visit to the cinema or for a drink. Some hit on the ingenious method of putting a pig in a trailer and towing it behind the car, so that if stopped and questioned as to their reasons for travelling, they could say, "I'm taking this pig to farmer so-and-so". The Police, the A.R.P. officials and military all could and did stop people to check on their movements in war-time. It was therefore necessary to have a plausible excuse. A farmer friend of my father boasted of having the best-travelled pig in Herefordshire.

Hitch-hiking was a more or less legitimate means of getting home for service personnel and anyone in fact who was anxious to grab a few hours away from the war; more of this in the next chapter.

CHAPTER FIFTY-SEVEN

Transport in War-Time Hoarwithy: Part Two

I mentioned hitch-hiking last month. As far as I recall it was a more or less recognised form of transport that everyone used from time to time. Most people were willing to give lifts, especially to service people. There was very little of the fear and suspicion that surrounds hitch-hiking today.

Service men and women, understandably, wanted to get away from camps, barracks, hospitals, etc., if only to get into town for a drink, or a trip to the cinema and of course, it could be wangled with or without a pass, a trip home. The gap in the perimeter fence was a feature of most establishments and friends could always be talked into signing-in for the absentee.

In Herefordshire (as elsewhere, I expect) the Army embarked on a programme to teach newly recruited A.T.S. girls to become transport drivers. The idea was that all those servicemen who had done the driving hitherto could then be released to go overseas and fight.

In those days the S.A.S. Barracks in Hereford was just an ordinary barracks called "Bradbury Lines" and it was from there that volunteers were sought to teach the girls to drive. I am told the entire regiment stationed there volunteered to a man!

However, as time went by, they quickly realised what an arduous and dangerous job it was and soon dropped out. Ultimately I heard the Army were advertising in "The Hereford Times" for civilian driving instructors.

Hoarwithy was very much involved in this, because one of the training routes went through Ballingham and Holme Lacy to Hereford. In the 30's and 40's most young girls had little or no experience of driving and those Army trucks were not the easiest of vehicles to learn on. The result was a trail of havoc and destruction through the village on all sides. The stone wall by the Church and opposite in front of "Evergreens" was knocked down and rebuilt several times and the wall in front of "The Harp" was hit so often I do not think they bothered rebuilding it for some time. Hedges, gateways and fences took a real battering. I think coming down the hill from Dewchurch must have been an ordeal for them and at the bottom they would take corners too wide or too short and Bang!...another bump!

The drivers instructing them would leap out and present the owner of the wall or gateway, with an Army Claims Form and in the end they had to carry wads of Claim Forms each trip.

The girls were often given a breather in Hoarwithy before returning to Hereford and they would come into The Shop or wander around the village. Some of them would wander up to the bakery at the back of The Shop and ask to use the yard toilet. This would present poor Walter Newport, the baker, with a dreadful dilemma. He always liked to be polite and helpful to the ladies and wanted to please, but on the other hand, it was part of his duties to empty the toilet-bucket and he did not see why he should have extra work to do because of visiting A.T.S. girls. What a dilemma!

Rumours began to circulate that the Army Instructors were suffering from stress and nervous collapse and were pleading to be sent overseas to fight rather than continue teaching the girls to drive.

My father related an incident that he witnessed one day. He said that one of the girls had got herself into an awkward position and was trying to reverse out of it. The instructor came and stood in front of her to guide her back, but she became confused and put the vehicle into first gear instead of reverse and drove into the poor man and pinned him up against the wall. He managed to instruct her how to reverse and free him, but he was white as a sheet and in shock. So perhaps the men were right to consider fighting in Africa as less hazardous than being driving instructors in Hoarwithy!

CHAPTER FIFTY-EIGHT

The End of The War

I think I have more or less covered the wartime years in Hoarwithy. The Allied landings in Normandy, the advances into Europe and the final surrender of Germany were, of course, closely followed by all. The "Buzz-Bombs" and V2 Rockets which came during the last year or so of the European war were a very real and horrible menace which effected those parts of England which were within their range, but Herefordshire was fortunately too far away.

The "Buzz-Bombs" were a sort of robot plane packed with explosives. They came across The Channel, towards London mostly and when their fuel ran out the engine stopped and they fell to earth; then "boom" another bomb. People would hear them coming and wait hopefully for them to pass on, but if the buzz of the engine stopped overhead, they would dive for cover and pray it would not land on them. The R.A.F. worked hard to try and shoot them down over the sea, or at least before they could drop, but sometimes there were too many of them.

Then the V2 Rockets started; they gave no warning. The first anyone knew of the arrival of a rocket was when it landed with an explosion. It was very unnerving as you can imagine. My Aunt, who lived in Acton in West London, said she was able to take ordinary air-raids and the "Buzz-Bombs", but found the V2's really got her down and scared the life out of her. I think the morale of the Londoners was really at rock bottom then. When the Allies finally overran the rocket launch sites, it was a wonderful relief.

When the German surrender finally came, the country went mad with joy. Street lights came on again and the sheer joy of being able to walk into a room and switch the lights on without having to draw the blackout curtains first was unbelievable. No more Air Raid Wardens yelling "Put that light out!" The relief was enormous.

After that I think we all thought, "Right, let's all concentrate on finishing off the Japanese War and get back to normal pre-war life again". The Japanese War was finished by dropping the Atom Bomb on Hiroshima and Nagasaki as you know and peace followed in the Far East. But of course, returning to pre-war conditions was not to be. Life had changed and moved on and there is never any going back in time.

PART THREE: Interval

CHAPTER FIFTY-NINE

The Birth of a Roving Reporter

In "Pax" I have tried to describe Hoarwithy as I remember it from the 1920's up to the end of World War 2. After that I was not here, because I married and went to live on Merseyside. I did not return here to live until the end of 1985, when my husband retired.

My parents retired here to Brae Cottage when my father sold The Shop and business in 1945. My husband and I visited regularly and we heard all the latest news from them. When we returned here to live at the end of 1985 and settled down and looked about us, I realised that the Hoarwithy I had returned to, had altered considerably from the village of my childhood and it has continued to change ever since. I had continued to visit old friends when we came here on holiday, so I had many ties with the old days. The Pragnells at the Lower Bibbletts, Austin and Jessie Baker at Tarrystones and Colin Eckley at the Bone Mill were some of these. Both the Pragnells and the Bakers are gone now, but Colin is still fighting fit, (Ed. Unfortunately, since this article was written some years ago, poor old Colin has now left us too, but well into his 90's!). My old friend Olwen Topping still flourishes and is far more convenient for the village comings and goings than I am.

My parents told me about the electricity coming to the Red Rail (Rhyd yr Heol) end of the village after the war. I think it must have been about then that the old S.W.S. Company was swallowed up by the M.E.B. and of course, with the electricity industry being nationalised, I do not think they had to pay to have the line extended to that part of the village.

My father fought hard to bring in the scheme for a Waterworks for this part of Herefordshire. He was a member of the old Ross and Whitchurch Rural District Council and they set this up. A borehole was sunk and a waterworks established to supply this area and householders had the offer to tap into the mains and have running water in their homes. A few people did regard it as an unnecessary expense, but when they found out that we had to pay for the scheme on our rates, whether we availed ourselves of it or not, they mostly agreed. So the mains water came to Hoarwithy in the'60's.

The next thing was refuse collecting. It must have given everyone great joy to be able to have their rubbish taken away for them, instead of having to burn or bury it themselves.

The biggest change in village life was the mechanisation of the farming industry, leading to the dwindling numbers of farm workers. This led to most of the cottages and many farmhouses being bought up by people not connected with the land. Most cottages have been modernised and enlarged and the occupants are either retired pensioners or town workers or self-employed in many different businesses. Quite a large number either use the cottages as holiday homes or commute on a weekly basis. This change has lead to a diverse population of many interesting people with a wider outlook on life.

The old village-style community tended to stay longer, to intermarry and to be more closely-knit and parochial in outlook. They were helpful to one another; everyone knew everyone else. As in all villages there was the usual modicum of gossip and scandal. We were an inward-looking group, I suppose and not much interested in the wider world.

The present-day Hoarwithy is still a community, but more loosely grouped. The tendency is for everyone to go out more; most young wives are independent and many work. In spite of this, I feel that there is a definite feeling of belonging to Hoarwithy and that in a crisis we would all rally round and act as a community. Village life has not died, it has altered and adapted to modern times and will I hope, continue to do so.

FOOTNOTE: "All Our Yesterdays" are now today!

I have been writing in Pax since Mr Enoch revived it in 1994 and appealed for contributors. My husband had written light-hearted articles for Pax up to his death and so when various people asked me to write about Hoarwithy's past, it seemed a good idea to continue the Cutcliffe tradition.

I have written about pre-war village life and then wartime and this month, I explained how I returned to the village. Now, where do we go from here? Should I;-

Go back to the beginning and tell about life as I remember it in the 1920 – 1940 period?

Retire gracefully (must be graceful!) from the pages of Pax altogether?

Try and think of something else to write about, (What, though?)?

Can you please let Mr Enoch know your views on the subject. I will do what people want, but please say something and do not leave me in suspense.

BETTY CUTCLIFFE.

To which Mr Enoch added the following note: (Editor's note. Betty is one of our most popular contributors. Her articles always reach me early, usually a month ahead of time. One option she offers, number 2, is not acceptable, but I hope readers will express their opinions in time for a result by the next issue of Pax in February (in by January 15th, please).

The result of the vote was for me to interview "old inhabitants". I wrote at the time:-

Christmas and Millennium celebrations are now behind us and the New Year is ahead. I have had some encouragement from Pax readers to go on writing about times past. One suggestion is that I do a "Roving Reporter" type of interview with any of the pre-war generation whom I can run to earth and see what interesting tales people have to tell me. I am willing to give it a try, but it will need a little planning and setting-up. This month I will write about cars.

CHAPTER SIXTY

Cars

My father needed a car to visit his customers. He would get around to all of them in turn doing a different area each day. He took their grocery orders for the current week, took the money from the previous week and talked about any new lines or special offers.

His usual method of buying a car was to attend a car auction in Gloucester and buy a good second-hand car which he would keep for about two years and then sell it and replace it with a newer second-hand car. Gloucester Car Auction was renowned throughout the West Country and was the place to go in those days. Mother and I would wait excitedly for his return and would admire the new car, ask for a ride in it and take great pride in it.

The first cars were of the Ford "Tin Lizzie" type. Big heavy things, they had lots of room in them. The top consisted of a canvas hood, which was hauled into place and fitted onto brackets. The windows were made of a celluloid substance and were slotted into place to keep the rain out. There was no heating and they were freezing cold and draughty in winter. Car rugs were a necessity, not a luxury. The headlamps were not very bright and night-time motoring was hazardous, although since there were very few other cars around, it was not as bad as you might think.

Running boards on the sides helped you climb into them, as they were much higher off the ground than today's cars. The engines were noisy and powerful and able to cope quite well with Herefordshire hills and the appalling roads, (you think you have troubles with mud and pot-holes today, do you not?).

As time passed the cars improved and proper saloon cars came along with wind-up glass windows, electric windscreen wipers, glass windows, improved headlights and so on.

I can remember a Vauxhall father had in 1936-38 which was a very nice car. Then in 1939 he acquired a Standard 8, green in colour, I think, which he drove throughout the war and beyond. It should have been changed for a newer model in its turn, but of course, by then the car factories were all geared up to building military vehicles and no new cars were being made. As a result no second-hand cars were for sale.

The bodywork on this Standard was showing signs of wear and tear. He had an encounter with a herd of frisky steers in a narrow lane and one of them pushed so hard on the car that he broke the central door pillar on the driver's side. The front door thereafter had to be secured with a piece of string. The driver's bucket seat broke and was held up with a brick under it and a thick cushion on top. The rear suffered from rust and father declared that he would not let mother sit in the back in case the rear fell off and he arrived without her. The engine still carried on and mother would reassure people by saying, "I know the bodywork is bad, but it has got a good engine".

Father had liked the Vauxhall and during the early part of the war had put his name down on their list for a new car. So when eventually, after the war was over and the car manufacturers were able to set up new production lines and then to acquire the steel to start making cars again, new cars began to trickle through onto the market. Hereford was allocated two new Vauxhall Wyverns. My father received one and he was so thrilled! His ambition to own a brand-new car had finally been realised. It caused a sensation! People flocked to look at it wherever he went. It does not seem believable now that there were no new cars at all until the early fifties and buyers were prostrating themselves before car salesmen and offering over-the-odds payments, but salesmen did not have any cars to sell! I suppose, looking back, that the fact that Britain was bankrupt had something to do with it.

Anyway, the final result was a very happy Mr Russill with his new car. To add to it, when he took the old Standard to Gloucester, hoping someone might buy it for scrap, he was delighted that it sold for £60. He had only paid £40 for it and he had run it into the ground for nearly ten or twelve years! New cars steadily increased in number after that and in a few years there were enough for everyone.

PART FOUR:
The Interviews

This is the first of my new-style articles. I am grateful to Frances Keogh of Kings Caple for help in preparing the interviews.

CHAPTER SIXTY-ONE

Rosie Townsend

I went to see Miss Rosalind Townsend of Hoarwithy who was most helpful. Her parents had six boys and herself. As Mr Townsend was a farm worker, they moved around quite a bit.

They first lived in one of the Ruxton Cottages. There were no "mod-cons" of course and their water came from a well down the road. Her brother Bill when very small, got out one day and was discovered peering down the well. Her mother was terrified that if she startled him, he might fall in. Fortunately she managed to retrieve him safely.

There was an old man called George Cooper who lived near them. His legs were very bad and he walked on two sticks. Mrs Townsend was very cross when one of her boys got behind Mr Cooper , put his head between the old man's legs and grabbed them from behind, causing him to fall over. He was not hurt but could not get up alone. She could not lift him, so at his suggestion she fetched a chair and he was able to cling to it and raise himself up.

The Townsends moved to Bromley Cottages and from there to The Oaks, which was a bigger place. The boys slept in one room which had two double beds and a single bed. Rosie had a small box-room to herself.

The next move was to New Mills, which is quite a large farmhouse, rather off the beaten tracks down a small road which branches off Laskett Lane and meanders across the county, to emerge near Little Dewchurch. Mr Roberts from Bromley Court (where the Day Nursery is now) installed proper plumbing for them, the water being pumped from a well in the house. They had a kitchen range, calor gas, etc.. The mains electricity did not come until after the war.

The farm had dairy cows, sheep and of course, a pig or two as they cultivated corn, sugar beet, etc.. Mrs Townsend made her own bread and made pots and pots of jam; they had lots of jam tarts and puddings.

They also had their own vegetables, home-cured bacon and milk, butter and cream from their cows.

I asked what Rosie could remember of Hoarwithy and she had to say, "Not a lot", because they all went to school at Little Dewchurch on weekdays and to Sunday School at Hoarwithy on Sundays. Other than that they had no need to come to the village. My father came once a week for their grocery order, which was delivered by van. They went occasionally to Hereford. They travelled by pony and trap or by bicycle to get around and from Fawley Station by train.

Hoarwithy Chapel flourished at that time. St. Catherine's Church did not run a Sunday School then, so all the children went to the Chapel. There were as many as 80 children in its heyday. Apparently my father used to go into the Chapel and light their oil heaters to warm it for them on Sundays.

Like me Rosie remembers Miss Mailes taking the Baby Class and giving us all toffee to eat and then Miss Nellie Williams taking the Girls Class. She was the maid from Prothither, where the Sherrats lived. They were one of the leading Chapel families. Their farm was later run by Michael Scudamore and is now the International League for the Protection of Horses.

The "Brethren" (as the worshippers were known, from "Plymouth Brethren") held rallies sometimes in the village. She could remember the big tent and going to hear preachers. Rosie remembered too, Sports Day and Fair which came every year.

One winter there was a heavy snowfall, followed by hard frost. The milk tanker could not get to New Mills and they had to get up to the road. When the tractor could not make it, they pulled and pushed a handcart up to the top.

During the war years they did not have any evacuees but were given help on the farm from the Prisoner-of-War Camp at Wormelow, (what is now the foxhunting kennels). Farmers were not supposed to ask the prisoners into the house, but most of them gave them a hot dinner in the back kitchen, when they had their own meal. Rosie remembers that they had German workers and soon discovered that German grammar was very different from English and some of the sentences came out in a very odd way which caused many laughs.

One of their workers was very particular about his clothes and asked for an overall to wear when Mr Townsend wanted him to help in spreading lime on the fields. The man looked at what was available and chose a wrap-around silky material that Mrs Townsend used when plucking poultry, because the feathers did not stick to it. The man was told he could have it if Mrs Townsend was willing. So he used it after promising to wash it. When he was reminded of his promise, he said in halting English, "I will help to wash your wife"!

At the age of 14 the children left school and went to work. They are now scattered around. Ivor, the eldest, lives in Australia. Geoffrey stayed at New Mills and took over when Mr and Mrs Townsend retired and went to live first at The Holt, eventually moving up to the bungalow where Rosie now lives. When Geoffrey himself retired, he moved to the bungalow he now occupies up the road from New Mills.

When Albert wanted to marry, he bought the land next to the Church and built himself a wooden bungalow, which has changed hands a couple of times since. The land was the vegetable garden to The Shop and Mr Topping was happy to sell it to him.

The Townsend family are all well and range in age from 85 to 70 years. A good record, I think!

CHAPTER SIXTY-TWO

Sport

I have previously mentioned that football and cricket flourished in this area pre-war and to a large extent, post-war also. As a girl, I was not involved and so do not have first-hand knowledge of events. Mr Enoch suggested that I should attend one of the meetings of the Age Concern Day Centre at Sellack Hall and talk to the members who had memories of sporting events of their era. So I went.

I was most impressed by the scope of Age Concern. A large number of people filled the Hall. All seemed happy and lively and were well catered for. As you might expect, the women outnumbered the men by about five to one. The men all sat at one table, so I was able to meet them quite easily. Colin Eckley was the only one I really knew; I have known him all my life.

Stephen Davies was a pleasure to talk to. He is 96 but does not seem anything like it. He had played both football and cricket, as had most of them. Some excelled more at one sport than the other, but all could play either. Lionel Howls, who comes from the Walford area and now lives in The Claytons at Bridstow, told me he used to play football for Hoarwithy at one period.

The Age Concern members had all been for a boat trip on the Brecon Canal the previous meeting; unfortunately the weather had been bad. "It rained when we started", they said, "and it rained all the time we were on the boat and it was still raining when we got back to Sellack Hall."

Stephen Davies was noted as a cricketer for spin bowling and he was a good batsman as well. He gleefully quoted to me, "Hoarwithy bullheads come to Caple, tip your hats". However the Hoarwithy team did win the cup just before the war. It was the Ross Football League they were in, they thought. Other footballers of note were Bill Bayliss of Pict's Cross and Roy Baynham of Sellack. I was reminded that Fred Mills, who died some years ago, told me that he used to run Fawley Football Club. He was a churchwarden at Kings Caple in the 60's or 70's and is remembered by many of you. Colin Eckley told me that Lady Densham, who used to live at Mount Pleasant, Hoarwithy, gave a cup for the winning team and Hoarwithy won it that year. Old Mr Williams from Llanfrother was a real football fan. He played in his young days and supported the team from the sidelines when older. He, it was who moved them from the field opposite The Salmons to the field behind The Harp and the Post Office, which is known as The Sports Meadow. This was a bigger and better field and more central to the village.

No-one could recall the story I had been told that Mr Williams shouted at the players so enthusiastically that his pony bolted and nearly tipped him into the river. The names of other old players were called to mind with great certainty. There was Tom Williams, the son of old Mrs Williams; Fred Moore, the son of the Kings Caple

Schoolmistress, Austin Baker at Tarrystones (from Tresseck Farm), who was married to Jessie, the daughter of Mr Williams, Llanfrother. In the Red Rail (Rhyd yr Heol) area there was Charlie Wooding, the Pardington family, Donald Jenkins, Reg Langford, Sid Harris and Bob Pember. At my end of the village there were Ernie Pragnell, who was a cricket bowler of renown and his son John. The list seems endless and it occurs to me that all the young men of the district played for their respective villages. There must be some young men who could start up the old traditions, if they wished. What about it?

Captain Evershed from Bromley was a cricketer and it was largely thanks to him that the cricket pitch in the Sports Meadow was laid out and I suppose, maintained.

Hoarwithy boasted a Tennis Club for a while on the meadow in front of The Mill. There were two courts and a clubhouse. It was wound up during the post-war years as there was no-one left to play. In its heyday it had a membership of about twenty. My father was keen on tennis and there were Nancy Adams and her stepmother from Withy Cottage, Violet Terry from Carey Post Office (the lady who ran the original Carey Telephone Exchange, now simply 840), Joyce Lewis from Harewood End and Neville Shaw from The Curatage. He, I remember, caused us some excitement and misgivings because he used a silk scarf to tie or hold up his trousers. It used to slip and we would hold our breath waiting for his trousers to fall down. (They never did!).

One of the Sellack members told me that there was a Rifle Club in Ballingham to which he belonged. Someone else remembered that Mrs Hilda Hardy and her sister Mrs Jessie Baker (wife of Austin), daughters of old Mr Williams, Llanfrother by his first wife, both played hockey and tennis at county level when they lived at Llanfrother after the First World War. Mrs Hardy had an impressive collection of cups and shields displayed in her cottage at Hoarwithy before she moved to Lawford House in Ross. Both sisters were first-class players.

Talk turned to other topics after they had finished with sport and Stephen Davies told us how he had charge of horses. As a waggoner he managed teams of carthorses when he was only a lad. Finally, I had to leave them, still talking.

CHAPTER SIXTY-THREE

Nora Williams

This month I had an enjoyable talk with one of Kings Caple's older citizens, Mrs Nora Williams of "The Firs", widow of Phil Williams of Hoarwithy. In the early 1900's, her family the Buftons, lived in Bosbury, a village about four miles from Ledbury. My father was an ex-Army friend of Frank Bufton, Nora's brother and went to Bosbury to work in the village shop there to learn the grocery trade. Then Frank and my father bought the shop in Hoarwithy and we moved there in 1921.

Nora was the first person in Bosbury to see me when my mother arrived home with me. She was also the first person to take me out in my pram around the village, so she has retained an interest in my welfare.

After schooling, she worked in London for about five years. She visited Hoarwithy to see her brother Frank and that was how she came to know Phil Williams. They married in the 1930's and lived in Hoarwithy and Kings Caple, eventually taking over the farm at Poulstone, where they lived until Phil retired. Then they settled down at "The Firs" where Nora still lives. Nora had no farming background but learned to make butter with a churn and how to manage poultry, how to grow and deal with fruit and vegetables and how to cope with curing bacon and all the other jobs which have to done on a farm. She loved helping at harvest time, stacking the sheaves into stooks and then seeing the threshing machine come to thresh the corn.

I asked her what she remembered of life in Fawley and Kings Caple. She recalled Mr Pritchard the landlord of The British Lion. (No more, alas!). He was an ex-Canadian Mounted Policeman and was full of ideas for increasing business. He pitched some Army Surplus tents in the field opposite and advertised them to townspeople coming on the train to spend summer holidays in Fawley. He had several chicken houses which he also let out as "chalets". Very enterprising.

Kings Caple was a very lively village with a lot of the activities centred around the School. Mrs Johnson was the head teacher then and she was always arranging concerts, outings, the Christmas Pantomime and so on. The bell-ringers were active in the village and they too had outings to the seaside.

The G.W.R. (Great Western Railway) ran a special excursion on Sundays to Weston-Super-Mare for the day, which cost five Shillings (25p). This was well patronised, as a day at the seaside was much enjoyed. The Mothers' Union flourished in Kings Caple and there was a W.I. in Hoarwithy which many Kings Caple women attended.

We talked about the weather next. Nora's chief memory was of a terrible blizzard in which Kings Caple was completely isolated and all the roads were so deep in snow that they could not get up to the village from the farm. Everything came to a halt. Many of the lambs died that year, frozen as soon as they were born and they were unable to reach many of the animals. When it was eventually cleared, the snow was piled up each side of the road like a cliff. The snow was followed by mild weather and horrendous floods. The low-lying houses down by the river were badly affected and Nora and Phil helped some of the families down there. The rain and floods were accompanied by gale-force winds and many trees were blown down which added to their problems. A large cedar tree in the churchyard came down. Nora of course, heard about the cloud-burst and flash flood up the Tresseck Valley, when the centre of Hoarwithy was flooded and the cows were washed over the wall onto the road opposite The Harp. Jim Oldis sent urgently to borrow Phil Williams' waders to get into the house to fight the flood.

I asked about war-time in Kings Caple and was told they did not have any evacuees or P.O.W. farm workers at Poulstone Farm, but they were sent five Land Army Girls from Perrystone. Kings Caple suffered from incendiary bombs, but they coped with these. Some also dropped on Hoarwithy Shop roof, but again these were extinguished without any major damage being done. A searchlight unit was stationed down opposite Milditch Cottage.

The main hazard was not bombs, it was the children at Poulstone Court. The house was taken over for a war-time home for disturbed children who could not be placed with ordinary families as evacuees. They were very naughty and did a lot of mischief. One or two of the older boys would climb out of the bedroom windows and get up on the roof until they were discovered. Since her husband died, Nora lives with her granddaughter, with her son nearby. She lives quite an active life refusing to sit around doing nothing. Long may she continue to do so.

(JC. Unfortunately, poor Nora passed on whilst I was typing this up, at the ripe old age of nearly 103!)

CHAPTER SIXTY-FOUR

Bill Harris (a)

This month I have been talking to Mr Bill Harris, who now lives in Hereford, but was born in 1939 in Stone Cottage, Hoarwithy (where Mr Stanley Pardington now lives). His father was then a Military Policeman at The Rotherwas Munitions Factory and because of the awkward hours of shift working he had to cycle to work.

In 1944 the family moved to the Church House and his parents took over the job of caring for Hoarwithy Church. His father cut the grass and kept the outside tidy. He also stoked the boiler. (The underfloor heating still worked in those days). His mother cleaned and dusted the church. Mr Sissons was the vicar then and he and his wife and sister-in-law lived in Hentland Vicarage (later to become Kynaston Court Residential Home). Mr Michael Evans took over next and was vicar on into the 80's. Mrs Gertrude Eaves from Underhill played the organ which was pumped by the Pardingtons, either Stanley or Sadie (there was no electricity for pumping air then).

Bill Harris says his father was paid £1-10s-0d (£1-50p) per annum for cutting the grass in the churchyard and received ten Shillings for digging a grave or twelve and sixpence for a multiple grave (that is 50p or 621/2p).

One year there was a landslide and some of the inhabitants of the churchyard nearly finished up on the road. His father had to help to re-inter several coffins. I remember my father writing to tell me that Walter Newport, our ex-baker, was left with his feet sticking out and had to be reburied. In life Walter was always complaining about his "poor feet". He suffered a lot from them and was always soaking them in a tin bath, when it was quiet in the bakehouse, so it seemed the final irony that he should also have trouble with them when he was dead and buried.

Mr Bill Harris told me about his neighbours, particularly the Prichard family from Altbough Farm and how kind they were: Ezzer (his name was Isaiah), Cliff and George and Mrs Thomas. The Harris family had many little gifts of eggs, milk, cakes, etc. from them. Jo Meale (son of Mrs Meale, also a Prichard), was known for breeding and training sheep dogs.

Bill reminisced about the Weaver family. We both remembered May, a charming and feckless young lady, who had a passion for a dashing young man with a sports-car and succeeded in having not one but two babies by him, which she left with the Nuns to be adopted. When asked why on earth she did not marry him and settle down, she replied that, "He did not believe in marriage"!

I may say there were some young ladies in the district who envied her ability to bounce back again all slim and pretty and resume life where she had left off.

Her sister Kathleen trained as a Red-Cross Nurse and joined The Navy as a V.A.D. and was a good nurse and was sent overseas. She and I bumped into one another in some Far Eastern country and had a heart to heart chat about Hoarwithy.

Their brother Bernard was only young then, but he later joined the Army.

Bill was educated at Hentland School with his brother and sister. Mrs Meredith was schoolmistress then. When the school was closed down, her daughter Margo and her husband were looking for somewhere to live and were able to buy it and convert it into a very nice home. Margo still lives there.

Bill played for Hoarwithy Cricket Club. Mr Douglas Roberts from Tresseck was a staunch supporter. He rented his field to them for a pitch and charged £25 per annum, but always gave the £20 subscription. They all missed him sadly when he died. Another tragic death was that of John Pragnall. John, like his father Ernie, was a good cricketer and played for Hoarwithy. He was vice-captain and then captain in 1963. Bill relates how a group of them had been at cricket practice and then walked around to The Harp for a drink. John just fell down and died on the floor as Bill walked in. This came as a truly dreadful shock to them all. John was only 39.

Many people supported The Cricket Club and they in turn played hard and competed against other teams from the area. Captain Evershed from Bromley helped with the pitch.

Lady Densham from Mount Pleasant, a very real lady in her ways, gave them a silver cup to be played for.

Eventually there were difficulties and the Club had to disband. Mr Austin Baker from Tarrystones wrote an article for The Ross Gazette which Bill has kept. Bill's father also played cricket and he followed on, as did most of the young men then.

CHAPTER SIXTY-FIVE

Bill Harris (b)

When Bill Harris was a boy there were a lot of children and young people around the village and there was a lot Bill remembered of their activities. As children they liked to play cricket in the road outside the shop, but the village policeman did not approve and tried to stop them. But Sergeant Moss (from Harewood End Police Headquarters) was all for it and told the local man that he should encourage sport. Bill remembers Sergeant Moss taking time and trouble to coach them and explain the game to them.

There was another policeman living along the Ballingham road later on, a P.C. Brooks, who had a large Alsatian dog called Bruce. There was a group of village boys playing under the bridge and they were able to walk along the girders to the stone piers. While they were larking about they spotted P.C. Brooks working in his garden and began shouting to each other about him, not realising how sound travels over water. When they noticed suddenly he was gone, one boy climbed up to look along the road. He was shaken to realise that he, the policeman, was waiting by The Toll House to catch them.They all hastily scrambled across to the Kings Caple side meaning to escape at that end, only to find Bruce sitting there waiting for them. So they had to surrender to the law and received a severe telling off.

When they were older, there was a young man called Ted Pyke, cook to Mr Wyndham-Smith of Aramstone. Ted was a little too fond of drink and the others decided to play a trick on him. So, after a heavy session they carted him off to church and laid him on the aisle floor and left him there. The church at that time had no electricity, but the underfloor heating was still working. So when Bill's father came in last thing at night to stoke the furnace, he got quite a shock to see, as he thought, a body laid out on the floor. In the light of his lantern, he must have thought it was a corpse! I think Bill and his friends were not too popular that night!

Cricket seemed to pop up again and again in Bill's tales of Hoarwithy. He remembered how the Hoarwithy team played Michael Scudamore's stable lads and Chapel played Church, "Saints versus Sinners"! He commented on Stanley Pardington being a fine athlete, good at running. This reminded me of Stanley winning an alarm clock for running at the Coronation Sports in 1937. Stanley was inclined to be a little late for work sometimes and this prize caused some hilarity.

Douglas Roberts, as well as arranging the cricket matches, used to organise trips and outings to the sea and take lads sledging when it snowed and was generally active in all sports and outings.

A gentleman called Mr Busby, a retired businessman from Birmingham and an ardent fisherman, used his energies to organise a library in the Reading Room and was helpful to the young people wishing to read and study. (He also lived along the Ballingham Road).

Dogs seem to feature in Bill's memories too. Michael Scudamore had a large Basset-Hound which accompanied him to cricket matches and caused a complete stoppage of play by sitting down on the pitch and absolutely refusing to budge.

Weather, a fruitful topic at any time, was discussed. 1969 was the year when a terrific cloud-burst up the Tresseck Valley caused a terrible flood. The water washed down in a great wave and swept through Tresseck farmhouse and on down the valley up to the level of the wall separating the field in front of The Mill from the road. The force of it swept the cows over the wall onto the road. The Mill, The Harp and The Aspens were all badly flooded and the aftermath of mud and rubbish was horrific. Tresseck Farm particularly must have been in a terrible state as the water scoured the cattle sheds and washed the manure into the house.

Then in 1976, came the drought, when everything was burnt brown and the brooks dried and the river sank so low that the gravel banks became uncovered on both sides. It was possible to just walk across in places. For the first time in years farmers experienced the problem of cattle actually straying across the river to the opposite fields.

CHAPTER SIXTY-SIX

Bill Harris (c)

Bill Harris and I discussed the people of Hoarwithy as he remembered them. Mrs Dance from The Mill was an obvious choice. When Mrs Dance was alive she was quite a personality and reigned supreme at The Mill (she had a parrot which bit my finger once and put me off parrots for years). After Mr Dance died, their adopted son, Jim Oldis, moved in to take over the running of the business. He and his wife Dolly had farmed at The Weaven in Little Dewchurch. Dolly arranged for Mrs Dance to occupy some rooms upstairs and the old lady made herself as independent as she could. They were both strong personalities with their own ideas of how to do things and so some clashes were inevitable. During one of her rebellious phases the old lady took to lowering a basket down from the upstairs window on a rope requesting passers-by to run errands to The Shop for her. This episode stuck in Bill's mind as he thought it very odd. He remembers how she eventually went on to live to be 100 and had a party with Queen's Telegram, Press interviews, etc.!

Bob Williams (brother-in-law to Mrs Norah Williams of Kings Caple) lived opposite the church and ran a haulage business. Bill told me that Bob would pack all the youngsters into a lorry and take them in to Hereford to watch Hereford United Football Team when there was a match on.

Hoarwithy had a dance band which played at many of the local venues (no discos in those days). They were called "The Jolly Boys". They went to Sellack Hall, Poulstone, Hentland School, The Red Lion at Peterstow, etc.. Mrs Heywood from Caradoc Court engaged them also.

The band was made up of Percy Oldis (Jim and Dolly Oldis's adopted son), Eddie Davies and Dennis Pardington.

Mr and Mrs Brewer from Fishpool were the next family he reminisced about. Mrs Brewer liked to go into Ross on a Saturday and enjoy life. Her husband used to come to meet the bus and escort her home. She was sometimes a bit merry and Bill remembers occasionally seeing him wheel her home in a wheelbarrow because she had passed out. Some while later poor Mrs Brewer was killed when there was a fire at their cottage at Fishpool.

In 1959 Bill Harris was called up to do his National Service. He subsequently married and went to live for a time at Sheppon Hill Cottage at the Hentland end of Hoarwithy. He and Hazel now live in Hereford. He says he has great affection for Hoarwithy and a host of happy memories.

CHAPTER SIXTY-SEVEN

Barbara Langford

This month I talked to Mrs Barbara Langford. Her parents, Mr and Mrs Owen started married life at Lower Bibblets next door to her aunt and grandfather. From there they moved to Middle Mills and then to Quarry Cottages, where I remember them. These two cottages, now renamed, are on the road below Quarry Bank House where Mr and Mrs Sorrel live.

Mr Owen worked at Tresseck Farm and they moved there to be nearer his work. He looked after the horses; all work on a farm was done by carthorse in those days. Most farm workers had Sunday off, but where there were animals, these had to be cared for. Barbara remembers her mother telling people with pride that Mr Owen was a waggoner and therefore received an extra six shillings a week. The standard wage was 30 shillings (£1-50) and he had this extra six shillings (30p) which made a big difference to the family finances.

Barbara had two brothers, Leonard, who joined the Royal Navy and Norman, who lives in Much Birch. They had a little sister, Betty, who died tragically at nearly five years of age. I have mentioned her before. She was taken suddenly very ill and rushed to Hereford Hospital. My father had one of the few phones and the Hospital rang him to tell the parents that Betty was very ill and they were to come in. Father collected Mr and Mrs Owen and took them to Hereford. The little girl died. They were never told the cause of death, only that she had an obstruction in her throat. (I always assumed it was Diphtheria). She was such a pretty little girl and much loved by everyone. Her sudden death must have been a terrible shock.

Barbara remembers the roads being repaired with stones, cracked up by old "Shelty" Harris of Forty Steps, the "Stone Cracker" and rolled flat by the big steam-roller. She thinks the weather was much colder in winter then than now, but there was more sunshine and less of the dull sort of weather we get today. She also remembers the Toll Bridge.

In 1947 there was a very heavy snowfall, followed by a sudden thaw and torrential rain which caused a bad flood. Quarry Cottages were flooded, as were many other houses on the lower slopes. That was the year that a lady was rescued from Aramstone Cottage through her bedroom window and ferried by punt across the fields to dry land. The Wye Valley was declared a disaster area and compensation was paid to those affected.

1947 was also the year that Barbara and Reg Langford were married and she went to live at Red Rail (Rhyd yr Heol) Farm. She had been nursing during the war years. When Reg died a few years ago, Barbara retired to her present home on Lascots Road.

Living conditions were hard. Water had to be carried from the river at The Bibblets and from the brook by The Salmons; at Quarry Cottages and at Red Rail Farm they had a well next door. Rainwater was collected in butts for washing. Her mother used the soapy water from washing clothes to scrub the kitchen step. They had the usual garden privy, but later had a chemical toilet. For lighting, they had paraffin lamps and candles and a lantern for outdoors. Electricity did not come to that end of the village until after the war. Her mother had a black-leaded cooking range and also a paraffin cooker for preparing food.

Like all cottagers they kept a pig and so had hams and bacon. When a pig was killed, they passed joints of fresh pork to friends and neighbours and in turn received the same. So pork was on the menu quite a lot. They kept poultry and grew their own fruit and vegetables.

Barbara attended Ballingham School for a few years and then went to Little Dewchurch. Hentland (Hen Llan) School at that time had large numbers , so Ballingham and Little Dewchurch with smaller classes were considered better. All the teachers in rural schools were good, hardworking women and respected by everyone.

Before the war, Hoarwithy had a general stores, a Post Office, a butcher and a weekly fishmonger. There was a cricket club, a football club and the tennis club. The young men of the village used to meet in The Reading Room (Barbara was not sure what they did!). There was an annual fair and sports day.

Kynaston House used to have rather smart dances, the ladies in long evening dresses and gloves, the men in their best suits. Hentland School sometimes used Kynaston House for functions. What a shame it was demolished. Barbara recalled the fire at Underhill in which the two Miss Pimbletts were burned to death. She also remembered the celebrations for the Coronation of King George VI (our Queen's father) and the Sunday School in The Chapel to which most children went. She enjoyed the outings which they organised.

The village was visited by "Gentlemen of the Road". There was a floating population of tramps, who would ask for some boiling water in their billycans to make tea. Most cottagers would give them some bread and cheese and a piece of cake. One in particular would offer to "sing for a few coppers". He had a terrible voice, so perhaps he was given something to shut him up! I think tramps walked from one workhouse to the next, which accounts for their continual movement on the roads.

Barbara's account of medical treatment is interesting. Her father had to go and fetch the midwife from Turkey Tump in a pony and trap, when she was born. Their doctor was from Much Birch, a Dr Mc Michael (Dr Mc Ginn's predecessor), but one did not summon a doctor lightly then, (he had to be paid!). Home remedies were used extensively. Elderflower tea was the cure-all. The flower heads were placed in a jug and boiling water was poured over them. One drank what one could and finished off the rest next day. It tasted revolting but it was good for helping sweat out a cold or fever.

Most country folk had a goose for Christmas and the fat was carefully poured into bowls or jars and kept in a cool place. It was used for chest infections, spread on brown paper and applied to the chest, covered with a cloth and fixed in place. This seemed to cure coughs and goose grease was widely used.

Barbara concluded by saying that whatever else could be said about country life then, it was never boring. When the men finished work there were always chores at home, feeding the pig, digging the garden, chopping wood or fetching water. The women had sewing, knitting, making rag-rugs, etc.. There was a lively social life with whist drives, dances and meetings, so that everyone was fully occupied.

CHAPTER SIXTY-EIGHT

Colin Eckley 1

This month I interviewed Colin Cameron Eckley. Colin is 88 years old and has lived most of his life in Hoarwithy and remembers the village from the early part of last century. Many readers will know him.

His childhood was unusual in that he was sent away when a week old to be cared for by Mrs Jones, a widow whose husband had died of injuries after a fall at work. She supported herself by caring for unwanted children. Colin's mother was unmarried and in those days it was considered a disgrace to the family. So he was sent away. "There was a lot of hypocrisy in those days", as Colin put it. His mother kept in touch for a short time only. She lived with her parents on a farm near Ross.

Since retirement, Colin has spent time at the Reference Library researching local history. He was surnamed Cameron and it was not until years later when he was in the Army and had to send for a Birth Certificate in order to marry, that he discovered that his surname was Eckley. This caused some commotion, as it was and is a criminal offence, to enlist in His Majesty's Forces under a false name. Colin had to go before his Commanding Officer and convince him that he was telling the truth. He was then taken before a Justice of the Peace to swear it on oath.

Mrs Jones lived at Stone Cottage (next to Hoarwithy House) on the Ballingham Road. She was a fine tall lady, who obviously cared well for her charges. (I remember her in her old age; she lived to be 93). There were two older girls and one boy a couple of years younger than Colin. Of the girls, one was killed, aged 82, knocked down by a car and the other lives in Canada, now 96 and still in touch with Colin. The boy grew up to be a big man, 6 feet 4 inches in height. He went to sea, did a spell in The Guards and then joined the Metropolitan Police. But he died of T.B. aged 26. He and Colin were very close. As Colin says, many young people died of T.B. then.

The Bone Mill was an old black-and-white house with the mill attached to it and sited beside the mill pond. This was cold and damp and very uncomfortable, I should think. The mill belonged to Tresseck and was called Tresseck Mill. But as it had been used for grinding bones for bone meal, it was also known as The Bone Mill and it is listed as such on the map of 1844. After Colin went there in 1921, it was only used for cider making or chaff-cutting. The mill was supposed to be haunted by the ghost of one Jack Sexty, who many years previously had been killed when his clothing was caught between a belt and one of the driving wheels on the main shaft. Sometimes the mill wheel would turn over on its own and folk said it was Jack working it to haunt them. Colin's opinion was that water leaking into the top trough would build up gradually until its weight would eventually force the wheel down and it would turn over once. This could be very disturbing if you were asleep in bed at the time.

Water was always a problem in the country and if you lived near a well or spring you were lucky. There was a spring further up the road from the Bone Mill and the brook ran past the door. The people of Red Rail (Rhyd yr Heol) had water problems and Colin was told that Prebendary Poole (who remodelled Hoarwithy Church) had also built a washhouse for their convenience near the river.

Sanitary arrangements consisted of the usual chamber pot in the bedroom and a building at the top of the garden. "Not very nice", as Colin put it, "if it was raining, snowing or freezing in the night". They had a fire with a small oven to one side of it for cooking and the usual candles, lamps, etc..

The 1914-18 war did not make much impact on Colin. He remembered men talking about it, but he did not understand what they were saying and he had no access to newspapers. Sir Henry Webb from Kilforge asked them all to a celebration when peace was declared and he remembers going there.

Hentland School was run by a Mr Thomas Hood, assisted by a young girl and all the Hoarwithy children of the day, about 70, walked there every day. If the weather was reasonable, they went up the path past Quarry Bank House and over the fields. When it was wet, they had to walk around by the road. If they were late they had the cane.

Boys and girls were seated separately and had separate playgrounds too. They were not allowed to eat their lunch inside unless the weather was very bad. There was some shelter in the playground. They had water to drink but were expected to bring their own sandwiches and bottles of cold tea. The boys used to clear off up the lane and light a fire to roast potatoes for themselves during the dinner hour. Boys wore short trousers and jerseys and thick nailed boots. Long trousers did not come into it until they left school and started work at 14.

"We did not reach a very high level of education", Colin said. I think Colin is to be congratulated for the way he has educated himself since leaving school.

The very first motorcar Colin had seen in the village, caused him quite a fright. He was quite small and minding his baby foster-brother in the pushchair whilst Mrs Jones picked some blackberries. Suddenly this noisy great monster came along the road towards him and he was terrified, he can still remember that quite clearly!

CHAPTER SIXTY-NINE

Colin Eckley 2

Hoarwithy was a thriving community with two grocer shops, a butcher, a slaughterhouse, a Post Office, flour mill, laundry, saddler, shoe repairer, stonemason, blacksmith, The Harp public house, a milkman, a bakery, a church and a chapel, not to mention a painter and decorator and builders. There was no need to go outside the village, but if you wanted to, there was a train service from Ballingham or Fawley to Ross, Hereford and beyond.

A Mr Chapman had a shop and a bakery adjoining The Mill. He had a large variety of goods for sale and had several delivery carts and a steam wagon. His business expanded to include a second shop (which was the shop I grew up in and which served the village and surrounding area for years). In Colin's opinion the poverty of the rural workers led to the closure of The Mill Shop and ultimately to Mr Chapman's selling the stores as well. Times were hard in the 1920's and many farm workers were on casual work. Many did not get paid if rain prevented work on the land. People settled grocery bills at the end of the week and if they could not pay, it was the grocer who suffered. Also I expect the flooding around The Mill was a hazard.

Mr and Mrs Tom Dance took over The Harp about 1900 and one of Colin's earliest memories is of Mr Dance coming out of The Harp and giving him a small packet of biscuits as he was wheeled past in his pushchair. The Dances kept The Harp for quite a time and then moved over the road to take on The Mill, which was working then, continuing for many years.

Originally there were five working mills up the Tresseck Valley, as shown on a map of 1754. New Mills, the least accessible, closed in the early 1800's; Prothither Mill closed in 1900. Middle Mills, listed as a Grist Mill at one stage, also closed. Tresseck, once listed as a Paper Mill, closed much later, leaving only Hoarwithy after the Bone Mill closed down. In Colin's view, Hoarwithy Mill being in the village, was much more accessible by road and was therefore able to carry on longest.

After Mr Chapman left The Mill Shop, it was empty and later used as a butcher's, run by Mr Tom Harry. Tom's father, who lived at Wye View, had a small dairy herd. His cowshed is now an office for the present occupant of The Salmons. Old Mr Jim Harry used to graze his cows on the roadside verges in the village. I can remember coming along the Carey Road threading my way between two or three cows. The verges were kept short and the cows were fed, so why not? (I shudder to think of today's juggernauts battling through cows!). He used to carry milk around to villagers in a churn and pour it into their jugs etc. as required.

Mr Romney and his son Reg did the boot and shoe repairs in the village. They lived at Red Rail (Rhyd yr Heol) as did Colin Price, our local painter and decorator

The Slaughterhouse was at the back of The Aspens. The method used was very crude. The beast was pole-axed and then had its throat cut. It was quite a busy place dealing with sheep and pigs as well as cattle. The meat was sold in the adjoining butcher's shop.

Upper Orchard and The Aspens guesthouses were run as one boarding house by the Mailes family and catered mostly for elderly people who lived in rooms as a permanent retirement home. Grace and Bertie Mailes could be seen frequently scuttling between the two houses carrying trays etc.! The Post Office was opposite the church gates then and run by a Miss Mailes, assisted later by her niece, Phyllis Williams. There was a postman called Mr Whiting who brought the mail from the train at Fawley and then delivered in Dewchurch, came back and collected Hoarwithy's letters, then returning the mail bags to the railway station.

CHAPTER SEVENTY.

Colin Eckley 3

The Blacksmith's Shop was next to the present Post Office and was owned by Mrs Pember, whose son worked it, helped by Mr Emery. They were always busy shoeing carthorses. Colin has quite a bit to say about the doctors. Both Ross and Much Birch Surgeries held a weekly session in Hoarwithy, at the Old Post Office generally. People thought twice about consulting a doctor then, because they had to pay. Epidemics of infectious diseases were common: measles, mumps, chicken-pox, whooping cough etc.. Diphtheria and T.B. were more serious and of course needed the doctor. There were deaths, usually of young people. The "fresh-air treatment" then current for T.B. was sometimes successful, but Colin thinks it was followed more to prevent the patient spreading it to other people than in the hope of a cure. The world-wide "flu epidemic" also spread to Herefordshire.

On a more cheerful note, the Annual Village Fair, held in The Sports Meadow, with running races, pillow fights, "bowling for a pig" and amateur boxing is remembered with pleasure, as are the Football and Cricket Club games.

In hot weather, Colin went swimming in the river. He comments that it was deep, swift and treacherous and one could only swim in certain parts. They used to go up by The Bibletts, where Colin says, years and years ago, the river barges used to load and unload.

The river meadows were lovely in his childhood, full of wild flowers and never ploughed. He could hear corncrakes calling in the long grass. After the hay harvest, the children were allowed to play in the meadows. The river swarmed with birds, swans, ducks, moorhens, geese, etc. and the water was full of fish. Large chub could be seen from the bridge.

Mr Wyndham-Smith lived in the old Aramstone House. This has been replaced and is the home of Miss Venetia Williams, the celebrated racehorse trainer, his great-granddaughter. Colin remembers the chimes of the stable clock (so do I and miss them). Mr Wyndham-Smith was a great salmon fisherman and still holds the record for the two largest fish caught in one day. One of them weighed 51lbs and the other 42 lbs. Casts of these monsters are still owned by Mr John Williams of Seaborne, his grandson. This wonderful catch was made on March 30th 1914.

Mr Wyndham-Smith was also a very good shot with a 12 bore and Colin admired his skill when he was sometimes employed as a beater at the pheasant shoots in Aramstone Woods.

Finally, Colin remembered Mrs Lewis, a widow, who ran her late husband's machinery business from the old Red Barn (long since demolished) on the Ballingham Road next to Underhill where David and Celia Gibbs live. She had a steam engine which worked a threshing machine (and I think a baling machine). She had a team of men who worked the machines and went around the farms doing the threshing and baling for the farmers.

On a personal note, Colin went away to The Army during World War 2 and met and married a lovely ATS girl in 1944 at the Garrison Church at Blackdown. His wife Gladys, died young in 1968 after a long illness. While she was ill, Colin had to go to work, but a good neighbour Mrs Iris James, who had been a nurse, helped Colin to look after her and she was able to stay at home until she died. June his eldest daughter, born in Doncaster, is married and lives near Weymouth. His second daughter Margaret, was born at The Bone Mill and has been a nurse at The County Hospital for many years. Pat now lives in Much Birch and Janet his youngest, has returned to live with him. Colin has seven grandchildren and four great grandchildren.

CHAPTER SEVENTY-ONE

Mr Simcox 1

By chance, I met Mr and Mrs John Simcox by the river. Mr. Simcox said that although he was not a resident now, he had great affection for Hoarwithy and promised to write down his memories for me.

It all began for him in 1930 when he was five years old. His grandfather Mr Randle Lunt, bought some fishing rights in Hoarwithy and the family spent a lot of their time here. At first he and his grandfather stayed at The Harp, run then by Mr Evan Jones and his wife. He recalls Mr Jones bringing hot water to their bedroom and having to wash there in a basin and then going down to eat a large breakfast. After that, off to spend the day fishing.

Mr Wooding the Water-Bailiff, had to be paid first for their day's fishing licence and his grandfather would walk down to Red Rail (Rhyd yr Heol) to see him and pay his dues. People were more honest in those days and would pay before starting to fish.

The Lunt family had a fishing hut by the river (they still have it). He remembers, "Grandad cooking meals for them in the hut". Mr Wooding used to patrol his beat along the river bank as far as The Carrots and he would call in on all the fishing huts en route. Mr Lunt would give him a drink, "a wee drop" and Mr Simcox thought he was probably offered a drink in most of the fishing huts along the beat.

The bridge was a toll bridge in those days and he recalls that to cross the river into Hoarwithy they had to pay. I think it a penny or tuppence for people and sixpence for a car.

They stayed in various cottages from time to time and when in residence his grandmother used to come and buy eggs from Mrs Harris at Forty Steps. He well recalls going with her, Mrs Dora Lunt, to visit there. Mrs Lunt always insisted that there were only 39 steps. Today of course, the whole layout at the front has been changed to allow access to motor vehicles and the steps have been rerouted at the side. But I can vouch for the fact that there are 40 steps; I have counted them!

A Mrs Kinderman-Walker lived in Mount Pleasant at the top of the hill on the Dewchurch Road at the time in the Twenties and Thirties and she owned a number of the cottages on the Carey Road. She was happy to let them, so the Lunt family moved around and stayed in any number of places as time went by.

Mrs Kinderman-Walker had a pump-house which pumped water up from the river to Mount Pleasant and was therefore able to supply water to some of the cottages. She also put in a roadside tap for the convenience of the people on the Carey Road.

Mr Simcox remembers staying at Marret Cottage (Mrs Cowell's home now) and also at my home, Brae Cottage. He particularly remembers the two-seater loo at the bottom of my garden (alas no more!). My parents used it for a coal-house with an Elsan in an extension to the coal-house. The lot has long since disappeared over the cliff in a landslide. We were too far away to share in Mrs Kinderman-Walker's water supply.

On another occasion the Lunt and Simcox families stayed at Quarry Bank (the Sorrell's home now) and of course at The Poplars, now called Upper Orchard and presided over by the Hurleys.

In 1938 Mr Simcox went into The Fleet Air Arm and old Mr Lunt, his grandfather died. Trips to Hoarwithy were not so easy for the family during the war years, but Mr Simcox had acquired a 1929 Austin 7 and when he was able to obtain petrol, he came here. He tried sleeping in the fishing hut, but found it very cold. He remembers lighting a candle which he burned all night and it provided some warmth. Later on he built himself a caravan on an old chassis. There were four beds, but they were very narrow, less than 2 feet in width, though he was able to get mattresses and bedding. He slept in a caravan, parked under the trees in the Simpkins meadow. The problem was sheep. They persisted in scratching themselves underneath the caravan and loosening the wooden boards on the sides. His parents only spent one night in the caravan and were so uncomfortable that they refused to come again.

CHAPTER SEVENTY-TWO

Mr Simcox 2

Mr Simcox's father tried to find other accommodation. Later on he put out a feeler to buy the Bridge Toll House. This had been used as a block-house during the war and would very probably have been demolished. The Council explained that they could not sell it, as it was part of the bridge, but would grant him a lease of 5 shillings (25p) a week for ten years and a further ten years at 7/6 (37 1/2p), if he would convert it back to a house.

The deal was agreed and he set about making it habitable. He asked permission to put a septic tank in the field below the house. That field is (or maybe was) the property of the church, as it was glebe land. The then vicar, Revd Michael Evans, refused on the grounds that there were more important things in life than a fishing lodge. However the Council allowed it to be sited on the roadside bank. The rainwater from the roof was collected in a tank which they used for flushing the loo. (It was very smelly, he recalls). They used river water for everything else.

Later on when his parents could no longer cope with The Toll House and gave it up, Mr Simcox looked around for somewhere else to stay and found that Hillside Cottage was for sale. It is the other half of the semi-detached Rock Cottage on the Carey Road. An old lady called Miss Matthews had lived there for years and on her death her nephew was offering it for sale for £525. Now Mr Simcox's sister had recently married and his father therefore said that as he had paid for her wedding, it was only fair to treat his children equally. He offered to buy Hillside and Mr Simcox took possession of it and decorated throughout. With the help of Mr Luffman, his next-door neighbour, he spent his holidays and weekends laying paths, making steps and so on, with the help of pebbles and gravel from the river and generally making it into a home.

In 1959 he got married and he and his wife lived in Birmingham, but came to Hillside for holidays and weekends. When the children arrived they all came. His wife was not too happy having to bathe the children in a tin bath in the kitchen, so eventually they added a modern bathroom and kitchen at the back of the house, built by the late Sid Harris.

In 1968 they sold their Birmingham house and moved down to live in Hoarwithy for three years, until they found the home they now own in Pershore. Those three years were a very happy time for them, as they loved Hoarwithy, but it was not without its drama. Mrs Gale who lived next door to them in Rock Cottage was stone deaf, elderly and definitely, as my son would put it, " a couple of sandwiches short of the full picnic".

When she was a young girl, Mrs Gale was a pretty blond who favoured pink satin, pearls, lace and frills, etc.. At this time she would appear in the morning in old clothes, a headscarf, no make-up and do her housework. In the afternoon she would doll herself up in a blonde curly wig, pink satin, loads of make-up and smile graciously at the passers-by. Sometimes she wandered off and got lost. The Simcox family had to send for the doctor or organise a search party for her if she was lost. They were very relieved when her nephew finally got her into a home at Ganarew.

CHAPTER SEVENTY-THREE

Mr Simcox 3

Many of the Hoarwithy people were recalled by Mr Simcox and he mentions Miss Lewis who took over her mother's business with the threshing machines, kept in the old barn, demolished now, next to Underhill. He remembers having yarns with P.C. Brooks (owner of the famous Alsatian dog, Bruce). Mr Brooks used to visit a Mrs Graze from Caradoc, who was bedridden and had an Australian husband who had an aircraft which he used to land on a nearby airstrip. (This caused some comments in the neighbourhood).

The Pritchard family from Altbough figured large in his memories and he mentioned particularly Joe Meale (son of a Pritchard lady). He thought Joe such a nice kind young man. He was asked once to hold an animal which Joe was treating for some injury.

Then there was the scandal of the Pennoxstone butler who stole the silver. He mentioned Sgt-Major Alford from Kings Caple and many other local people whom he had known. In Hoarwithy itself, of course, was the village's centenarian, Mrs Dance. He remembered the business of her lowering a basket from her window to ask passers-by to buy things for her. Apparently, she liked a drink and this method of buying it from The Harp, was to outwit Dolly Oldis who strongly disapproved of alcohol!

We also spoke of the tragic drowning of his neighbour Ralph Luffman. The Luffmans lived in an unpretentious little bungalow, since demolished to make way for Wyehurst House. Ralph suffered a mental breakdown, which was successfully treated in hospital and he came home only to have his wife suddenly taken ill with a strangulated hernia. She was rushed off for emergency surgery. He thought she had cancer and would not return and so walked out and disappeared while the river was in flood. His body was not found for over a year and poor Mrs Luffman was left alone to watch the river flowing past. My mother helped console her and all the village was relieved when he was finally found and could be properly laid to rest. She was then able to go and live in Newport near her god-daughter.

Mr Simcox went to work for a firm called Wilkinson and Puddell after the war. He says he must have been to the Village Shop many times, but could not remember meeting either my father or Mrs Topping there. But he did remember bumping into Mr Pierson who was embarrassed to find he had a load of ladies corsets to sell in his car.

Hillside is still in his possession and his own children, now grown up, come and stay there from time to time, as do he and his wife. As he said, he does not really live in Hoarwithy, but he has been associated with it all his life and feels very much part of it.

CHAPTER SEVENTY-FOUR

John and Anita Brooke 1

Most of the readers of Pax know John and Anita Brooke of Kings Caple. John is a churchwarden and Anita is the organist.

When, as a young bride, Anita first entered Pax country, she was immediately knobbled by the then vicar to come and play the organ in church. She has been playing church organs ever since. A big "Thank You" to you both for all the work you do.

John came originally from Much Birch of a farming family which moved when he was a little boy to live at Prothither Farm (now home to the ILPH, the Glenda Spooner Farm). John started at Much Birch School and then from Prothither he went to Little Dewchurch School. In his later years at Little Dewchurch he undertook the task of delivering the school milk. (How many readers remember the little one-third-of-a-pint milk bottles which were issued free to every young child in the land at one time?). John said it was hard lugging all the bottles up to school every day.

When the war broke out John was 14 and so had to leave school to help out on the land. He also took on the delivery of milk in Hoarwithy village.

In 1944 the family moved from Prothither to Ruxton Farm and then in 1950 his parents bought a farm in Madley, leaving John to run Ruxton Farm on his own. At this stage Anita comes into the picture, as they were married then.

Anita came from Aconbury. She lived in a red-brick house on top of the hill looking down on Hereford. It was situated where the parish boundaries of Aconbury, Dinedor and Bullingham all point together. It must have been nice to have a house on the junction of three parishes. She went to school in Bullinghope and then to Hereford High School for Girls.

John and Anita both went to Little Dewchurch "ChurchYouth Club" where they fell in love. They were married in 1950. They lived at Ruxton and had a happy time. Their family consisted of two girls, Esther and Susan and their son Elwyn. John recalls that he acquired an ex-Army Jeep at this period and used it to get about. They were good, strong, handy vehicles, just the thing for driving around a farm. But they had no bodywork to speak of, no doors, no roof, etc.. John says the children loved riding with him around the fields and he scandalised some of the ladies in Hoarwithy who could see him across the river with three children and usually a couple of dogs as well, careering around the fields. They were convinced that the children would fall out! However, they did not, so all was well.

After about ten years they moved to Lower Penalt as the Aramstone family wanted to move into Ruxton. They were at Penalt for 30 years. Then, leaving their son to run it, they went to Seven Acres, where they are now.

I asked them what they remembered about the roads and John told me of seeing the side road which goes from Prothither up to the Dewchurch Road at The Weaven being resurfaced with blue stones. The roadman cracked the big blue stones up into little pieces and spread them over the surface and rolled them in. It does not seem believable to us now that stones for road mending were tipped at the roadside as big boulders about 12 inches in size and that the local roadmen cracked them up into small pieces by hand.

We talked then about the basic mod-cons of the houses they had lived in. Prothither had a well for the water supply and outdoor toilets, whilst Ruxton had indoor toilets and the water supply was pumped by a windmill. All lights were candles and paraffin lamps; cooking was done on a range and a bread oven. There was no electricity in those days.

CHAPTER SEVENTY-FIVE

John and Anita Brooke 2

If the doctor was needed, he was called from the Post Office telephone in Hoarwithy. Later on of course, most farms had phones installed. John and Anita lived as most farmers did and still do. John cultivated the land and grew grain, potatoes and sugar beet etc.. They grew fruit and vegetables, kept cattle, sheep and poultry. It was mostly horse power in the early days, but by 1947, tractors began to appear and as time wore on the tractors took over on the farms and the horses faded away. This speeded up the farm work considerably.

For recreation, John played football and cricket for village teams and enjoyed the sports at the Hoarwithy Fair. Whilst at Prothither he attended Hoarwithy Church and sang in the Choir, as did Colin Eckley, Charley Wooding, Sam Romney and his son Reg. When the Brooke family moved over the river, they went to Kings Caple Church. There were plenty of church outings, picnics and fetes, pantomimes and so on, all of which the Brookes enjoyed. John recalled going to Hentland Vicarage (now the Kynaston Residential Home) and to Pengethley when Major Curling lived there and a summer fete where there was ice-cream (a Stop-Me-and-Buy-One fridge) and balloons filled with hydrogen. I had never seen these balloons before and kept mine in my bedroom for ages until it deflated. Ice-cream was a real treat to us all then, because no electricity meant no freezers nor fridges and therefore no ice-cream. For travelling around it was either bicycle or walk; for further away bus or train. Very few people had saloon cars then.

During the war years John's parents were given two girl evacuees; one of them was taken home again immediately by her parents, but the other stayed a long time. John remembered a girl called Betty Mills who was billeted with the Powell family and a boy called Rigby. They stayed for some time, but he did not think there was much contact post-war and he does not know what became of them.

He remembers the air-raids. One bomb landed in the grounds of Poulstone and two on Ruxton land and of course, he heard all about the bomb which damaged Kilforge House and also the incendiary bombs, aimed at setting fire to the corn harvests. These incendiary bombs did not start any big fires and did not do much harm, except for the one which landed on the roof of Hoarwithy Shop. This one was extinguished by my parents with a stirrup pump before it caught hold on the roof beams.

The weather was a subject on which the Brooke family had plenty to say. In 1947 there was a very heavy snowfall which blocked the roads in Kings Caple and then everything froze and caused a lot of difficulty and hardship. There were 13 deaths in Kings Caple that winter. John was called out on several occasions to use his tractor to collect coffins from the railway and take them to the bereaved families and also to take the coffins away again to await burial. A man living in the riverside cottage below the railway bridge was taken ill and needed the doctor. Again John was called in to help. He took the doctor on his tractor to the station, where the doctor boarded a train which stopped on the embankment above the cottage, enabling him to get down to the cottage from the railway line. The snow was followed by a rapid thaw, which of course caused terrible flooding. The floods probably caused the collapse of the railway bridge beyond Fawley Station at the end of Penalt Farm. This was the occasion when Eddie Davies heard a crash and went to investigate. He saw what had happened and was able to rouse the Station Master at Fawley in time for him to phone through to Ross and so prevent the early train from leaving for Hereford with factory workers. The flood waters weakened the pier on Hoarwithy bridge, next to the Toll House and the bridge had to be closed for a time for it to be repaired. This caused much inconvenience as you can imagine!

CHAPTER SEVENTY-SIX

John and Anita Brooke 3

The cottage by the river, below Aramstone House, was two cottages in those days. Although they are close to the river, they are actually on a small mound and normally above flood level. But on this occasion the water came in up to 3 ½ to 4 feet (just over a metre). Mrs Meale, one of the Prichard family from Altbough Farm lived in one cottage and Mr Moat, the retired gardener from Aramstone House, lived in the other. Ted Harris from 40 Steps had a boat, so he and John Brooke and Joe Meale, Mrs Meale's son, went to the rescue.

Mrs Meale climbed out of the bedroom window and Mr Moat insisted on coming out of his downstairs window and got wet-through in the process. Anyway they were rescued and the "boatmen" were the heroes of the hour.

Mr Lunt's fishing hut on the Ballingham Road was floated away during the flood and was found stuck in the hedge by the approach road to the bridge. This road was also flooded between the Ballingham Road and the bridge. The hut was retrieved and towed back and firmly anchored down.

As a contrast to the floods, we talked about 1976 and the great drought. It was one of the driest summers on record. There was no rain at all for several months and the river became very low, with gravel banks on both sides. In places it was so shallow that one could walk across. Farmers experienced the problem of cattle straying into fields across the river, an event which normally never happens.

John told me that some beasts from Ruxton crossed over and got onto the road in Hoarwithy. They wandered up the lane by Quarry Bank and one cow became separated from the rest and wandered onto the flat corrugated-iron roof of a hillside garage. The roof gave way and dropped the cow down fair and square between two cars. She caused extensive damage to both cars and was firmly stuck. They had a fine job extracting her. However, the insurance company nobly paid up for one garage and two cars, so it could have been worse.

On the subject of things getting stuck, I was told about Ted Pike, who has appeared before in these tales of past adventures. This time he came home in a fuddled condition due to too much ale and he fell over on a cattle grid and got stuck between the bars. Once more John Brooke was called upon to help. He says it was a real problem trying to extricate him, as one can imagine, as he was firmly wedged and too fuddled to help his rescuers.

Anita talked about the Romneys, old Mr Sam and his son Reg. They lived in Hillcrest on top of the hill at Red Rail (Rhyd yr Heol) (where Mrs Hardy lived for many years) and they repaired all the boots and shoes belonging to everybody for miles around. They often delivered the repaired footwear and she remembers seeing them walking around Kings Caple with bundles of boots and shoes.

John recalled "Bengatha" the Village Hall in Hoarwithy. It was a privately-owned building and the name was made up out of the initials of the shareholders. It probably would not pass the buildings regulations today, but it served its purpose and lots of organisations rented it for dances, concerts etc.. The whole of Hoarwithy village had a lunch there to celebrate the Coronation of King George VI.

We agreed that life has changed greatly since our young days and hope that this has given Pax readers some idea of what life was like.

CHAPTER SEVENTY-SEVEN

Mr Tom Chamberlain 1

I had heard that Mr Tom Chamberlain had had an interesting life, so I visited him. He started life in Pembridge, where his family were living when he was born. His parents and two brothers moved on when he was a baby, so he does not remember it. His sister was born at Nantmel near Llandrindod. His father was a gardener, who learned his trade at the old Kings Acre Nursery in Hereford and worked on various estates and big houses all over Wales and Stafford. Therefore Mr Chamberlain said he started school at five and left at fourteen but he went to so many different schools that he was never really able to form lasting relationships.

He thinks the weather was colder in winter in those days, with hard frosts and snow, but less rain, bright starry skies at night and in summer, hot dry weather. There was no mains water; they went to wells, sometimes a walk away from their cottage. He particularly remembered one with frogs and newts in it. Roads were the same as here, stones and no tarmac. The toilets were down the garden and candles and paraffin lamps were used for lighting, with cooking dependent on paraffin stoves or on the fire.

His parents kept goats both for milk and sometimes for eating. They had chickens for eggs and occasionally to eat. They shared a pig with a neighbour. Cow's milk was available, but usually involved a walk to the nearest farm, sometimes quite a long walk. For fruit and vegetables, since his father was a gardener, they usually had an agreement with his employers, so they were well provided for in that respect.

Some of the villages where they lived had a shop and a public house, but no village hall that he could remember and no annual fair either. There was mostly a church, but often quite a distance away and they walked there. Sometimes there were Sunday Schools, but he did not experience any Sunday School outings. For going farther away, he remembers an occasional train trip, but it was mostly walk or a ride in a pony-and-trap or bicycle if you were lucky.

I asked about the doctor and he said, yes, they had access to one usually, but often four or five miles away. He had the usual childish ailments and his brothers had bronchitis from which he successfully recovered.

The farms around were much as farms everywhere at that time, cattle, sheep and growing crops. It was mostly horse power then; there were horses everywhere.

When he left school, the family were living in Newcastle-under-Lyme and he went to work for a firm which was laying pipes for the hospital. The pipes were all laid in a trench and his job was to cover them all with tar before the trench was covered in. It was a very messy job and he got more tar over himself and his clothes than he did on the pipes. His mother was not best pleased and so his father managed to get him a gardening job instead. At that time, his father worked for Meakins, the china people, at their big house. His mother also helped by doing washing for the family. He remembered that they had a dog which jumped up and tore a big feather quilt which his mother had hung out to dry. The dog ripped a piece out and scattered feathers all over the place. He does not know how the Meakins reacted, but he imagined they were not pleased.

He married in 1934, when the family were living in Pembrokeshire and he then went to Clyro (or at least, near there) and was there when war broke out. They had three evacuees, a brother and two sisters from Bootle: Colin, Bernard and Betty Brodie. They were nice children, who eventually went home and he lost touch. This was not surprising, as he was called up in 1940 and sent overseas in 1942. He spent five years in Egypt, Italy and finally Germany, eventually returning to Catterick. In 1946 he was finally reunited with his wife and they went for a time to live with relatives in Fownhope.

Chapter Seventy-Eight

Mr Tom Chamberlain 2

Not surprisingly, Tom made up his mind that he wanted a home of his own. As he explained, tied cottages left you always at the whim of your employer who could throw you out of both your home and your job with very little notice. He heard about the new council houses being built in Kings Caple, so applied for one and was allocated his present home. He settled there and has remained there ever since.

He looked around for work and in 1950 he started with the railway. He began at Holme Lacy. He had to cycle there every morning to be ready for the first train, but he and his bicycle came home by train to Fawley. Later he was able to work at Fawley. He started as a porter and had quite a lot of jobs to see to. His main function was to keep the station clean and tidy and deal with the general public. The first thing was to light the fires in the Waiting Rooms and Ticket Office and to sweep and dust and clean the rooms. Then the platform had to have the stone edging clean and whitened on the train side and the gravel had to be raked. There were some flowerbeds to care for and the banks to be trimmed. It was his job to issue tickets, carry baggage and help the passengers.

All the lighting was by paraffin lamps and they all had to be cleaned, filled and lit after dark and in the early morning. Tuesday was the day that the lamps on the signal gantries had to be changed. The old lamp was removed for refilling etc. and new lamps were put in their places. You needed a good head for heights doing that job, as it was necessary to climb up to the signals and then across to the "arm" to replace the lamp.

As well as the passenger side of the station, the porter was responsible for the goods and parcels, which came in the luggage van. He had to book in and out all the varied goods which came through the station. Parcels had to be weighed, labelled and dispatched on the right train and charged the correct price. He spoke of the famous bridge collapse when a bus service was laid on for passengers travelling between Ross and Fawley, which of course made extra work for him.

As well as the passenger trains, there was a daily goods train. Tons of sugar-beet went by train to Kidderminster and milk to the Cadbury's Factory at Leominster and live cattle, sheep and timber to various places. Products such as coal, building materials and so on, came into the goods department and probably the freight side earned more money than the passenger in the heyday of rail transport. When Mr and Mrs Fyshe settled in Sollers Hope, Mr Fyshe sent all his animals and equipment from his previous farm by rail to Fawley and then transported them all to his new farm. Mr Pritchard from the British Lion Pub, which flourished in those days, (alas no more), ran a pony-trap to transport goods from the station to their destination in Fawley, Kings Caple and the surrounding area. Mr Eddie Davies who had a mobile

shop then, used to have a box of fish sent to him each week by rail and Lad
Cockburn used to collect a fish frail every week from the station (a salmon?); sh
would come for it in a chauffeur-driven Rolls-Royce and always tipped the Porter
two-shilling piece.

Sometimes Mr Chamberlain was sent as a Relief Porter to other stations. H
worked at Mitcheldean and at Longhope and remembered hampers of plums goin
by rail in the autumn from Longhope Orchards.

Mr Whiting the Postman used to meet the early train for mailbags and woul
deliver to the Post Office. He would then come through to Hoarwithy Post Office o
his bicycle and up to Little Dewchurch. After a rest he would return and empty a
the boxes and take the letters to Fawley to catch the trains back to Gloucester c
Hereford. The Ross-Hereford line was only single-track, but Fawley Station had
passing place, i.e. two lines with two platforms so that the up and the down-lin
trains always had to wait for each other there, so that they could pass safely. Fawle
was connected to the Signal Boxes at Ross and Rotherwas and had a signal syste
which ensured that two trains never met head-on. The driver carried a big key whic
he handed to the signalman on exiting the single-track section. When the next trai
arrived going in the opposite direction wishing to use the single-track section, the ke
was inserted into a socket and the connecting plunger was pressed. This rang a be
in the next signal box. When that box acknowledged this bell by pressing the
plunger, it unlocked the socket to allow the key to be released which was then hande
over to the engine driver. The signals could not then be altered until the train cleare
that section of track and handed the key over to the second signal-box. Keys wer
later superseded by a sort of metal tablet.

(JC. Having consulted the Signalmen at Severn Valley Railway, I gather the
system is similar, but differs in one respect, namely, the fact that after the "be
ringing" they indulge in a bit of "code breaking" as well! They send through a coc
which consists of "3, pause, 1", which is repeated at the other signal box, but the
is held longer and whilst it is being held, the key can be released at the other end.
gather too that the significance of "3, pause, 1" is that this code represents
passenger train; if it were a goods train a different code would be used).

CHAPTER SEVENTY-NINE

Mr Tom Chamberlain 3

Mr Chamberlain was promoted to Signalman when Mr Wright, the previous Signalman, retired. An Inspector of Signals from Gloucester came out and examined him and made sure he was competent to carry out his duties. I can remember a minor panic at Fawley Station when a sow with a litter of piglets got onto the line and was hastily chased off just before the train arrived from Ross, so I asked Mr Chamberlain if there were any accidents in his time. He said that thankfully there were no human accidents, but it was a problem with cattle getting on the lines sometimes and that in the dark, there were occasional collisions where cattle were killed.

When the goods train came it would often have to pick up or drop off a wagon or two and this involved shunting backwards and forwards. The shunting sidings were on the tunnel side of the station, where Mr Randall has his motorcar repair business now. A wagon would be pushed out onto the main line by the Shunting Engine, which would push it up to the train of wagons and the men would drop the coupling hook into place, this in the Hereford direction. If a truck was given a push from the Engine, it would run down to join the train by itself, because the line sloped a little towards Ross and it was easy to couple up when it connected. However, one day the truck must have been given an extra hard push and the Guard had not put his Guard's Van's brake on very firmly. When the truck hit the main line-up of trucks, it started the whole lot going back down the line and everyone was running after them applying the brakes on each truck.

There were two porters and they worked a shift system, 7 am to 3 pm and 2pm to 10 pm approximately. The Station Master was in overall charge and attended to the running of the Station. He did not perform menial tasks, such as issuing tickets or manhandling parcels.

Quite a lot of livestock travelled by rail and there were strict rules laid down for them. Dogs travelled in the Guard's Van and had to wear a muzzle. Poultry had to travel in a cage, big enough for them to stand up in. Pigeons came in baskets, sometimes with instructions when to release them. The time, weather, etc. had to be recorded for the owners on an official card. Cattle and other stock had to be fed and watered, if kept overnight; young calves had to be given a drink.

Regarding the present controversy over "leaves on the line", Mr Chamberlain said this was never a problem for them, in spite of all the trees growing along the Ross-Hereford line. The problem which did concern them was frost. This caused the joints to freeze and not move when the Signalman pulled the lever which controlled them. To avoid this happening it was necessary to put salt on them. This had to done hourly in freezing weather. Railway maintenance was sometimes the cause of

143

rerouting express trains onto single-line tracks like Ross-Hereford, which of course did not stop at Fawley. Then the Porter had to stand on the platform holding the signals key with the loop sticking out for the train to grab as it flashed past. The train driver was responsible for handing in his key in exchange. Sometimes he would just drop it on the platform as the Engine rushed past.

I must confess that the intricacies of shunting and signalling were rather beyond me and I think it is wonderful that Mr Chamberlain can remember the times of all the trains and where they originated from and went to. Sadly, in 1964 Mr Beeching closed the line and sold off all the rails, sleepers, ballast and so on and it is hard to realise where the line used to be.

Mr Chamberlain was not out of work for long (about a fortnight) and he started a new career as a storeman at Wiggins factory in Hereford, where he worked until he retired. Wiggins was an engineering firm from Birmingham, who opened a branch in Hereford post-war.

Mr Chamberlain had to open, examine and check all in-coming goods and document them and then do the same in reverse to all the goods being used in the factory. He commented on the big rolls of glass-fibre which used to be stacked up right to ceiling height and containers of acid, originally in big carboys and then in plastic containers. He confessed that it worried him in case the glass got broken or the plastic punctured.

The factory had a branch line, which came right into the factory premises and really heavy stuff was unloaded by crane. There were also tankers which were left on a siding. Apart from that there were lots of smaller boxes of parcels of all sorts of things.

It seems obvious to me that Mr Chamberlain held a very important and responsible job there, keeping track of these goods. Sadly his wife died and his daughter now looks after him. They have a nice snug home and a very big garden which, as you might expect, looks well cared-for. I hope he has many more happy years to enjoy it all.

Betty Cutcliffe (Née Russill)